The Flame-Haired Dynamo

Mick Martin

SAMUELFRENCH-LONDON.CO.UK
SAMUELFRENCH.COM

MUSIC USE NOTE

IMPORTANT BILLING AND CREDIT REQUIREMENTS

THE FLAME-HAIRED DYNAMO was first presented at Hull Truck Theatre on 28th November 2013. The performance was directed by Nick Lane and designed by Pip Leckenby, with lighting by Graham Kirk, illustrations by Kev F. Sutherland and original music by Tristan Parkes. The cast was as follows:

CHRIS MCCANN	James Weaver
DEBBIE MCCANN/JULIE MCCANN	Fiona Wass
SGT CRADDOCK/MR SELBY/GRANDAD	Roy Castleton
TITCH MCCREAVIE/SIMON/ DEWHIRST/IAN MCCANN	David MacCreedy
JACKIE/FIONA GARBUTT	Catherine Lamb

FOREWORD

British adventure comics reached their peak in the post-war years and
thrived right into the 80s, before the computer came along and all the
world of XBox and Playstation took over. But prior to that the *Dandy*
and *Beano*, *The Victor*, *Hotspur* and *Tiger* were the weekly treat, and the
Christmas annual took pride of place under the tree each year. There
were characters like Alf Tupper – Tough Of The Track, or Bernard
Briggs, the best amateur goalkeeper in Britain, and his motorbike, with
a bathtub for a sidecar. One of my own favourites was Sergeant Pilot
Mike Braddock VC, a tough, no-nonsense sort who refused promotion
to the officer ranks because he didn't want to be one of the nobs and
rubbing shoulders with the brass. The subject of class in British society
was a recurring theme of many of the stories.

The British comics were less about superheroes who could fly or had
amazing powers; the heroes were much more ordinary blokes, working
class characters not unlike your dad or granddad, people you could
recognize, people like you. Alf Tupper was an orphan, as was Bernard
Briggs; he would always triumph for the little guy against the posh nobs,
and then go have fish 'n' chips. *Billy's Boots* is the story of Billy Dane,
who finds an old pair of football boots that once belonged to forgotten
1920s striker, Dead Shot Keen. When he dons the boots Billy magically
transforms from being rubbish into a hotshot striker.

It was only when I read back through the old annuals I realized that
women and girls were virtually non-existent, unless they were a doting
mum or gran, or the football star's doe-eyed girlfriend who hangs on
his arm and doesn't say much. The comics reflect a boys' own world
that shapes us to this day. Besides being a lot of fun to create and write
my very own comic book hero, albeit on the stage, this seemed like very
fertile terrain for a play.

The central character in the play is Christopher McCann who has a
lifelong connection to Titch McCreavie, aka the Flame-haired Dynamo!
Titch is an amalgama of all the above characters, the kid from the
orphanage who made it to the top playing for his local team, Felsworth
Rovers. But in real life Christopher is a man in crisis: he's lost his job and
struggles to relate to and understand his wife's point of view. He runs
away, to his attic, his childhood actually, and hides in his old Venture
comic annuals.

As Christopher reads the comics now, and even enters the world of
them, he brings his own world along. Things begin to change in the
usually perfect world of Titch McCreavie, and especially his doting
girlfriend, Jackie. Meanwhile a second character is introduced, Sgt
Craddock, leader of Craddock's Commandos, an all-action war hero who

is always fighting the Germans in the Ardennes Forest. Craddock is that no-nonsense tough guy Christopher used to aspire to be, but never was. Through the comic stories, Christopher begins to make sense of his own youth and childhood, and how it has affected him ever since. It proves to be a cathartic journey all round.

The original production in Hull owes a great deal to the wit and shared enthusiasm for the comic world of Nick Lane. It was his idea to have screens onstage for comic panel projections to support the action and reinforce the comics' visual style. This helped to deepen and reinforce the world of the comics visually, to depict other characters mentioned, such as dastardly Bruddersford Rangers defender, Digger McGhee, and the filthy rich 53rd Earl of Southsea who not only owns Southsea Hotspurs but is also their star player. The speech bubbles referred to in the text can either be projected onto the screens, or they could be read aloud by Christopher as it is through his reading and imagination that we initially enter the comic world.

Above all it should be colourful, fast, fluid and fun. Just like the comics.

Mick Martin, April 2014

CHARACTERS

CHRIS MCCANN

DEBBIE MCCANN

JULIE MCCANN

SGT CRADDOCK

MR SELBY

GRANDAD

TITCH MCCREAVIE

SIMON

DEWHIRST

IAN MCCANN

JACKIE

FIONA GARBUTT

ACT ONE

Scene One

The stage is an attic room, steps leading up from the sub-stage into the space. It will double as **CHRISTOPHER**'s *childhood bedroom later. There is also the requirement for some vestige of late 70s family living space. Nothing else ought be naturalistic. The attic is full of boxes of old books, records, stuff of all sorts. We hear all manner of argument and hullabaloo raging below.* **CHRISTOPHER MCCANN**, *a man in his forties, suddenly appears through the hatch, followed by his wife,* **DEBBIE**, *same age.*

DEBBIE. All I'm saying is that a little bit of appreciation for my situation wouldn't go amiss.

CHRIS. Look you work in all this corporate carry on, you know the drill. I'm not actually unemployed, the last place *restructured*! They restructured me, you know, like a cubist painting. Left leg out of my shoulder.

DEBBIE. Head wedged sideways up your arse.

CHRIS. Precisely. Oi!

DEBBIE. Then get real. Laid off is laid off.

CHRIS. Just before Christmas and all.

DEBBIE. It was two months ago!

CHRIS. You're right, just before bonfire night, never mind Christmas! Double cruel!

DEBBIE. I'm running the house, paying the bills *and* doing the housework, and all I'm asking...

CHRIS. Feels more like a demand.

DEBBIE. Suggesting, coaxing… is for you to pull your weight.

CHRIS. I cooked dinner last night *and* did the washing up.

DEBBIE. You put two pizzas in the oven.

CHRIS. *And* took them out again. Don't underplay the achievement.

DEBBIE. And the dishwasher did the pots.

CHRIS. Ah, but who loaded it? Who switched it on? He shoots, he scores. Believe it or not, Deb, I do still have my dignity.

DEBBIE. And we still have our bills to pay.

CHRIS. Aye, and as we all know, when the bills come through the door…

DEBBIE. Somebody has to pay them! Maybe Titch wot's'is-face could help?

CHRIS. In what way?

DEBBIE. By going to the car boot sale?

    CHRIS *goes to the image of Titch.*

CHRIS. You can't get rid of this, I've had it since I was a kid!

DEBBIE. I wasn't just talking about the poster…

CHRIS. Never. Don't worry, Titch, I won't let her hurt you.

DEBBIE. Look, while you're lurking about up here like a sodding hermit in the lost temple of boy-land, we are looking at Christmas with no money to spend.

CHRIS. We've got the kids' presents already.

DEBBIE. And everything else? My mum, aunties, uncles, friends' kids? You're alright; everyone belonging to you's dead and gone already, but I've got a shedload and…

    CHRIS *picks up a copy of 'Venture Annual'. For the first time he opens it, and as he flicks through the pages so comes in a soundscape of all the different stories, it drowns out* **DEBBIE** *as she speaks. The sound of machine guns and artillery as* **SGT. CRADDOCK** *bellows "Eat lead, Fritz!" followed by "Go Flame-haired Dynamo!" as* *the football crowd roars. Then an elephant trumpets as we hear 'Jackson Of The Jungle!', an aeroplane whines and 'Sky Falconer – the only female daredevil of the skies!' He closes the book. Neither speaks for a second.*

Are you even listening to me?

CHRIS. Yeah, course.

DEBBIE. What was I saying?

CHRIS. That I am the light of your life, the cream on your cake, the—

DEB. The pain in my arse! I was saying you could get a fortune for all this on eBay. That'd sort us out.

CHRIS. eBay?

DEBBIE. Other husbands would.

CHRIS. I aren't other husbands.

DEBBIE. I aren't the DSS, or Mother Theresa.

CHRIS. Look, I aren't saying I'm perfect. Come on, then, name names, who are these top of the range husbands who take their wives here, there—

DEBBIE. Exactly, restaurants, cinemas, weekends away.

CHRIS. Buy 'em this, that, the other.

DEBBIE. What? Dinner now and again?

CHRIS. Laugh, joke, flick easy banter across the dinner table.

DEBBIE. And not be a miserable git with a face like Grimsby all the time, yes! Look, I don't expect presents or jewellery, but maybe just take us all out for the day?

CHRIS. I took all of you to Flamingo Land!

DEBBIE. Oh not that again!?

CHRIS. That place… means a lot to me.

She looks at him, then around at the comic book paraphernalia etc. that is all around the room. She starts to go through it.

DEBBIE. What do you see in this stuff?

CHRIS. Poetry. It's a forgotten world.

DEBBIE. Ask yourself why? *Craddock's Commandos?*

CHRIS. Sergeant Craddock, the Ardennes Forest, 1944. Magic!

Enter **SGT. CRADDOCK,** *in WW2 fatigues.*

CRADDOCK. Nazi Stormtroopers at three o'clock! Take cover!!

We hear Germans yelling in a comic style and see projections of them on the screen as **CRADDOCK** *opens up a volley of machine gun fire.*

Eat lead, Fritz! Take that back to old Adolf for Christmas!

Exit **CRADDOCK.** **DEBBIE** *is looking at Titch stuff now.*

DEBBIE. And the Flame-haired Dipshit.

CHRIS. Dynamo! Careful, that's issue four! *(reading)* "Follow Titch McCreavie's rags-to-riches rise from the orphanage of industrial Felsworth to the summit of the English First Division!"

Enter **TITCH MCCREAVIE** – *the Flame-haired Dynamo. He has a shock of red/ginger hair and around his neck is his silver locket. He does his stretches and his exercises. The movement quality should reference the visual essence of the comic frames, at all times.*

TITCH. Cor blimey, Mr Selby's given us a stonking training session today! Only nine more miles to go! Still, we'll be fit as flamin' fiddles for the packed Christmas fixture programme!!

Exit **TITCH.** **DEBBIE** *is still reading, shaking her head in bemusement.*

DEBBIE. The only smoky old *northern* town with its own nuclear submarine port, international airport, space station, RAF base! All they need is a Harvey Nichols and it tops the lot.

CHRIS. It's an escape. It's like life, only, minus all the awful shite that ruins it.

DEBBIE. What like, work, women?

CHRIS. Who is it watches soap operas and *Dancing on Ice*? What's real about any of that? Glass houses, missis?

CHRIS takes the comic from her and puts it on a different pile. She picks up another.

DEBBIE. For God's sake, you're a middle-aged man!

CHRIS. OK, don't rub it in. Look, before computers took over the planet like the bloody daleks and enslaved us all, this was what kids had! And it was real, Debbie! Thursday afternoon there'd be a queue at the shop for it, kids'd be getting withdrawal, doing turkey like soddin' heroin addicts, until they got their hands on it, Deb! The feel of it, smell of it... the weekly fix.

DEBBIE. Oh for God's sake! The *smell?*

CHRIS. Oh yes. It's a physical sensation! I'm telling you. They're art.

DEBBIE. They're shite!

CHRIS. The art and literature of the common man!

DEBBIE. *(to the heavens)* Arghh!!! I despair!!

CHRIS. Believe me, Deb, when I was a kid, I didn't just read this stuff... I was *in* it!

He picks up a comic, shows it to her, takes out the locket as he speaks. It takes her attention.

Here we go, 'So, you want to be a top player...

As CHRIS shows her the article, TITCH jogs back into the space and jogs on the spot as he repeats the advert.

TITCH. ... like the Flame-haired Dynamo, do you? Well just send six Venture comic tokens and 79p P&P for your own replica lucky locket and you'll be running out beside me for Felsworth Rovers in no time!'

He raises his hand, football-hero style, and exits. CHRIS hands DEBBIE the comic, she peers at it, confused.

CHRIS. Back garden, I used to put my lucky locket on... 'McCreavie on the left, knocks it inside to McCann, he beats two men, shoots – oh, what a goal!'

He mimes shooting and then raising the arm to salute the adoring masses. She ignores him completely.

DEBBIE. Christopher, are some of these new?

CHRIS. No. 1970s, all of them.

DEBBIE. I mean new to you? Now?

CHRIS. No.

DEBBIE. Why are they still in packaging then? What's this?

She lifts a **TITCH MCCREAVIE** *lucky locket from the package.*

CHRIS. That's Titch's famous lucky locket! I showed you it.

DEBBIE. You showed me the *advert*...

CHRIS. Yeah, no, see, I used to have one... but... I lost it, so...

DEBBIE. So you bought another? When did these arrive?

CHRIS. A while ago.

DEBBIE. When?

CHRIS. Just the, er... few weeks... days... back... *(pause)* Yesterday.

DEBBIE. Yesterday!? You better be having me on? *(pause – no response)* Christopher?! I'm struggling to keep a roof over our head, and you've bought this crap?

CHRIS. It's not crap! This is the 1978 Christmas Annual... and... I told you about '78, didn't I? It was a rough year for me, one way and another.

DEBBIE. How much were they?

CHRIS. Not that much, really... in relation to...

DEBBIE. To...? What we owe on the house? Trident nuclear deterrent? Look, just tell me the truth. I won't be mad. How much?

CHRIS. 100 quid.

DEBBIE. *(shrieks)* What!?

CHRIS. Each.

DEBBIE. You are having me on!? You have got to be having me on.

CHRIS *says nothing.*

You are *soo* divorced! Christopher!

CHRIS. I… you don't understand, Deb… saw 'em on eBay… started bidding… then couldn't stop.

DEBBIE. No, I don't understand! You are dead right. I don't understand you at all.

CHRIS. Look, I'll get a job scrubbing floors if I have to.

DEBBIE. I keep thinking you're going to wise up, but… it's my own fault, isn't it? It's not like I haven't been told you're a waste of space.

CHRIS. Oh? Let me guess. Simon.

DEBBIE. Don't make this about me.

CHRIS. Well, come on, what's the great oracle's opinion then, in between taking you for a spin in his new car…

DEBBIE. I shouldn't have told you that.

CHRIS. Skiing trips, golf weekends…

DEBBIE. He's a nice bloke.

CHRIS. He's a dickhead.

DEBBIE. You're pathetic. At least he wants real things from life! And I tell you, it's nice to be listened to from time to time. Plus, for your information, Chamonix looks lovely.

CHRIS. Just looks cold to me. Give me Felsworth any day, thanks.

DEBBIE. You're like a child, Chris, and you need to sort it out! Are you coming downstairs or are you going to mess about up here in Felswick?

CHRIS. It's Felsworth!

DEBBIE. I don't care!

*Exit **DEBBIE** angrily.* **CHRIS** *puts down the comic he was holding, heads to the exit, stops, sees the annual, and picks it up.*

Scene Two

CHRIS is reading the annual. He sees the locket, and without thinking puts it on.

Enter **TITCH MCCREAVIE**, *blowing from his training run, followed by* **MR SELBY**, *in sheepskin coat, trilby hat, pipe, he always has this costume.* **SELBY** *and* **TITCH** *animate; the image of the changing room in the background.* **SELBY** *is holding his pre-match team talk, there is a board for tactics, but all that is on the board is an image of one man, Digger McGhee.*

SELBY. We've trained extra hard this week specially to keep the Christmas pounds off with all that lovely posh nosh you'll be scoffing over the holidays!

TITCH. Yikes, boss! I luv me Christmas posh nosh, turkey and trifle.

SELBY. No turkey and Christmas pud, Titch! Not if we're going to get promotion. Felsworth Rovers into the English First Division.

TITCH. Every footballer's dream, Mr Selby!

They hold a tableau image of wise old boss and young player, both grinning.

CHRIS reads from the annual.

SELBY. Now, I'm expecting a tough match today boys. Bruddersford Rangers are our arch rivals, so a win today is vital! If we mess up, there'll be flippin' riots!

TITCH. You don't need to tell us, boss. Not after last season.

SELBY. I remember, nobody likes tear gas.

TITCH. Or tanks. It was a feisty one alright!

SELBY. I want you to keep an eye out for Bruddersford defender, Digger McGhee.

TITCH. Digger McGhee! That hatchet merchant?

SELBY. Yes, and since you made him look a fool earlier in the season, he'll be after one man, Titch – you!

TITCH. Crikey! Digger McGhee, the only man with more suspensions than the Felsworth suspension bridge!

CHRIS. *(reading)* 'Which links the bustling industrial town of Felsworth, with the rural county of Flatcolnshire!' Continued next issue. Brilliant.

CHRIS puts the comic down. SELBY and TITCH freeze. CHRIS stands, as if ready to go downstairs, then looks at the next comic on the pile.

Ah sod it, read on!

He gets the next issue and opens it. Now we create an action sequence from the comic. The game is created in a series of tableau comic images, which need not be immobile but which carry the essence of the visual comic style. The sound of the crowd comes in.

CHRIS. It's late in the game and Felsworth are trailing one-nil to Bruddersford Rangers.

SELBY. Come on, lads! We can't lose to this lot!

The following are speech bubbles which appear on the screen. CHRIS reads them.

1   Pacy wingman Howie Haddock's makes a break down the line!

2   Titch is in space the box!

TITCH. Great work, Howie! On me bonce, mate!

CHRIS. Howie hits a harpoon of a cross!

The roar of the crowd comes bursting in as we see TITCH rise and strike the pose of powering the header into the net.

1   Titch McCreavie bullets a header past the stricken keeper!!

2   What a goal!

3   Go Flame-haired Dynamo!

4   Titch will you marry me!?

TITCH. Come on, Rovers! Two minutes left; we can still score the winner!

SELBY and CHRIS speak simultaneously; CHRIS supposedly reading from the comic.

SELBY. That's the spirit, Flame-haired Speedster!

CHRIS. Titch McCreavie is taking on the entire Bruddersford team on his own!

TITCH. Just their last defender to beat...

SELBY. Titch, look out!

Screen image of the dastardly moustachioed Digger McGhee, the moment the boot goes in! TITCH collapses.

TITCH. EEAUURRGHH!!

SELBY. Blimey! That's a free kick in a dangerous area! The flippin' ref's waved play on!

CHRIS. On the touchline! It's Titch's girlfriend!

Enter JACKIE. She wears a scarf, has wavy hair, blue eyes and lovely eyelashes.

JACKIE. Get your hands off my Titch!

CHRIS. The whole stadium draws it's breath is Titch injured!?

JACKIE. What have they done to him?

CHRIS. Is this the end for the Flame-haired Dynamo!?

JACKIE. Oh, Titch, I love you!

TITCH gets to his feet dizzily, his legs wobbling.

TITCH. Huh!? Blimey... Wot... wot 'appened?

JACKIE. Oh, Titch, I love you!

TITCH. Now's the time I need my dead grandpa, old Whiskers McCreavie. Help me, Gramps!

Image of ghostly GRAMPS, in kilt, tartan hat etc. TITCH holds the locket around his neck. CHRIS does the same with the replica.

GRAMPS. Always remember, wee man, if you can't use your noggin – use your speed instead!

TITCH. Yikes! Crikey, Gramps! I won't let you down! While there's still a chance to save the day!

Now there is cheering and hurrahs etc. The following calls come from the crowd and appear as speech bubbles. **CHRIS** *reads them.*

1   *Bruddersford striker, Whiplash Wilson breaks away!*

2   *But look at McCreavie go!*

Whiz lines on screen! Titch in running pose!

SELBY. What a player!

JACKIE. What a guy. Oh, Titch… I love you!

SELBY. They've hit it! It's beat the keeper!

TITCH. But… not… me!

1   *He made it!*

2   *Cleared off the line! Incredible!*

The final whistle sounds out. The conversation from the crowd continues.

3   *There goes the final whistle!*

4   *Well played Flame-haired Dynamo!*

MR SELBY *and* **JACKIE** *now join* **TITCH**, *as if post match, he has the ball under his arm.*

SELBY. Great goal Titch. Pity we couldn't get the winner.

TITCH. You ain't kidding, boss. Cripes, if I ain't about to score when that great clunking clod McGhee sends me into blinkin' orbit!

JACKIE. How could he?!

TITCH. Hey, babycakes, the Flame-haired Dynamo's made of strong stuff.

JACKIE. Oh darling, I just worry about you, that's all. I sit at my desk at Felsworth International Bank – on the 48th floor of the new skyscraper, Felsworth Towers, thinking about you.

Image of perfect girlfriend gazing/smiling at her hero.

CHRIS. If only.

Scene Three

CHRIS *is mucking about with Christmas lights when* DEBBIE *shouts from below.*

DEBBIE. *(off)* I'm back!

There is the sound of laughter from below. He knows what the laughter means.

CHRIS. Oh. Great.

More laughter.

(shouting off) Everything all right?

DEBBIE. *(off)* Yeah, fine. Simon's here.

CHRIS. *(as Simon)* 'Hi, buddy. What's new?'

SIMON. *(off)* Hi, buddy. What's new?

CHRIS. *(to himself)* Nothing. You're here again. And still a cock.

He slumps into the chair again. Takes another comic from the pile.

Achtung Achtung! Gott im Himmel!! Here we go.

There is a sudden crack of machine gunfire and lights going crazy with shell burst, the sound of aircraft whirring etc. CRADDOCK *enters.*

CRADDOCK. Eat lead, Fritz!

CHRIS *is reading his comic.* CRADDOCK *is part of his story.*

'Ere, kid, get your perishin' head down, this is serious!

CHRIS. You're not wrong.

CRADDOCK. We're deep behind enemy lines, kid!

CHRIS. Also true on a great many levels.

CRADDOCK. This blinking forest is swarming with Germans! Okay, I'm about to bust into the secret bunker of Count Otto von Gorschnitzen of SS Intelligence.

CHRIS. I remember, except now he's called Simon and he manages a UK-wide firm of computer systems designers, sales and service…

CRADDOCK. Same perishin' kraut wot tied me to the wheels of his Panzer Super Tank!

CHRIS. I remember!

CRADDOCK. On the count of three, use every grenade you've got. Blow that stinkin' squarehead to smithereens!

CHRIS. Oh, if only!

Enter **DEBBIE**. **CRADDOCK** *freezes in comic panel frame of square-jawed action hero!*

DEBBIE. Are you stone deaf?

CHRIS. No. I hear every word of it.

DEBBIE. I must have called your name five times.

CHRIS. Well, between defrosting a chicken, switching the washing machine on, the thrilling daily job search and getting the Christmas lights untangled… you just get so… into it.

DEBBIE. Oh you poor thing! It must be exhausting for you.

CRADDOCK. Cover me, boys, I'm going in. Take this, Count Otto!

CRADDOCK exits. SIMON enters.

SIMON. Room for a little one?

CHRIS. Simon, come in, fella, *great* to see you…

SIMON. Chris, hi, always a laugh.

CHRIS. What is?

DEBBIE. I invited Simon to join us for a bite to eat.

SIMON. If that's okay with you?

CHRIS. Not really…

DEBBIE. Any problem, is it?

CHRIS. No no no, the more the merrier.

SIMON. *(looking round)* So… you're a comic man. Same as myself.

CHRIS. Really?

DEBBIE. Really!? Oh no.

SIMON. Yeah. Well, used to be, but... more a Marvel, Superman, Batman type, you know.

CHRIS. They're DC. Not Marvel.

DEBBIE. Who cares?

SIMON. Right. Right. Sure. Sure. Sure. Sure. And these are...?

CHRIS. ... old school British adventure stuff...

SIMON. Genuine working class heroes, eh Chris?

DEBBIE. Don't set him off, please. *(to* **CHRIS***)* I thought Simon might be able to help.

CHRIS. With?

SIMON. Sorting those lights first off, buddy. Here, let's have a look...

> **SIMON** *gets busy.* **CHRIS** *doesn't look too happy.)*

DEBBIE. Getting work.

SIMON. Happy to help. It's tough out there unless you're prepared to challenge yourself skills wise. Are you getting any responses?

CHRIS. Er... well... few irons in the fire, you know.

SIMON. Nothing then?

CHRIS. Not a sniff, no.

SIMON. Have you thought about online shopping?

DEBBIE. Not if he wants to keep his balls.

SIMON. They hire extra people up to Christmas, in the warehouses.

DEBBIE. There you go! You'll be McCann of the Amazon... Online Bookstore!

> **DEBBIE** *laughs. No one else does. The Christmas lights go on.* **SIMON** *has fixed them.*

DEBBIE. Aha! Brilliant!

CHRIS. It's only lights.

DEBBIE. You couldn't do them.

CHRIS. I was doing them!

DEBBIE. No you weren't! When I came up here you were reading a bloody comic! *(to* SIMON*)* Sorry... we shouldn't let our petty squabbles...

SIMON. No, no it's fine. Really. My wife and I broke up recently... and I don't know, I miss this.

CHRIS. What, arguing cat and dog?

SIMON. It's more than that, though, isn't it?

DEBBIE. Rarely.

SIMON. It just makes you think.

CHRIS. What about? Alcohol? Self harm?

SIMON. You know, you can spend ninety grand on a car, live in a beautiful house, go skiing on Boxing Day with mates... but it doesn't mean that much without what you've got.

CHRIS. An interesting hobby? I get you.

SIMON. You know what I mean. I'll get going. Listen, guys, Christmas drinks... I'd love to have you over. Christmas Eve? Really get the festive season off with a bang?

CHRIS. Well, truth is we're fairly...

DEBBIE. Looking forward to it already.

SIMON. I'll text you, times, details, dress codes... and Chris, I'm sure you'll get something soon. I'll see myself out. Bye, Chris.

CHRIS. Cheers, yeah. Great to see you! Take care!

SIMON. Sure.

Exit SIMON*,* DEBBIE *looking daggers at* CHRIS.

DEBBIE. Thank you for making me look a complete idiot!

CHRIS. Be fair, you helped.

DEBBIE. My boss comes here to offer you advice in your quest for employment and what do you do? Act like a teenager. Be careful, you'll be out in spots again!

CHRIS. All right. One: I don't need his advice in my quest for anything, and two: he didn't come to help me. If you can't see it I can; he's pretty much asking you on a bloody date right here in my house!

DEBBIE. Don't be ridiculous! You need help, and quickly!

CHRIS. Come over for Christmas drinks to my massive house. Look at all my ski equipment and golf trophies, while I flirt with your wife! Sure, sure, sure!"

DEBBIE. He's a nice guy.

CHRIS. He's a knob.

DEBBIE. Why? Because he prefers people to comics? Because he'd rather spend time with me than in bloody Felswick?

CHRIS. It's Felsworth.

DEBBIE. I couldn't give a shit where it is!

Pause. **DEBBIE** *is quite upset.*

DEBBIE. You know you need to decide where your priorities lie, Chris... either with me or Titch Ma-soddin'-Creavie!

CHRIS. Look... Debbie, that's not true...

DEBBIE. It's how it feels.

CHRIS. Come on...give me a break! I have no job and going round to his so I can feel even worse than I do already...it's not my idea of fun.

DEBBIE. And this isn't mine. I'm going in the bath. Are you coming down to sit with your kids, or are you going to stop up here in 1978 again?

Exit **DEBBIE** *angrily.* **CHRIS** *looks round. His comics are out of their piles.*

CHRIS. Oh bollocks.

Music. Time passing. A sequence. **CHRIS** *putting on a dressing gown, going up and down the stairs,* **DEBBIE** *coming up to the attic with wrapped presents, a dumbshow argument,* **CHRIS** *reading more comics and so on.*

Scene Four

It is now Christmas Eve. **CHRIS** *is sat in his dressing gown with a can of lager and a comic. Enter* **TITCH** *trotting on the spot at the end of a training session.* **SELBY** *follows, holding an umbrella. Thunderclap.*

SELBY. This has to be our year, Titch... promotion!

TITCH. Yes, Mr Selby! Felsworth Rovers in the First Division!

SELBY. I remember the first time I saw you.

TITCH. Back when I was just a cheeky nipper? Playing sock football, amid the fires, up and down Felsworth slagheap with the other kids from the orphanage.

SELBY. I knew straight off you could make it in the modern game.

TITCH. What got my goat, there was a perfectly good pitch at the posh snooty school what the nobs go to next door. But they wouldn't let us little toughs from the orphanage on it!

SELBY. I know. It was my idea.

TITCH. What? Mr Selby?!

SELBY. I did it for you, Titch. Don't you see?

TITCH. Huh? No.

SELBY. Running barefoot, over those scorching hot coals!

TITCH. Ah! Now I see! Cor blinkin' blimey! Genius, Mr Selby!

SELBY. It gave you the extra *pace* that's vital in the modern game!

TITCH. Stone me, boss! That's why I'm so fast as what I am! Getting over them scorching hot coals without burning my tootsies off! Thanks, Mr Selby.

Enter **JACKIE** *in some distress. She runs to* **TITCH.**

TITCH. Hey Jackie, my little Miss Marzipan!

JACKIE. Oh Titch, thank the stars!

TITCH. Hey babycakes, what's up?

JACKIE. It's the bank!

SELBY. What about it?

JACKIE. It's being robbed at gunpoint!

SELBY. What?!

TITCH. Not again!?

JACKIE. Yes!

> **DEBBIE***'s voice is heard from below. The characters freeze as she speaks.*

DEBBIE. You going to be much longer?

CHRIS. Five minutes…

> *The comic characters animate once more.*

JACKIE. They're demanding a helicopter, they've got almost £90,000 in cash!

SELBY. Ninety *thousand*?! But that's –

TITCH. The money we raised for the orphanage with that charity match!

JACKIE. They're loading it into bags right now!

TITCH. Cripes!

JACKIE. Yes!

TITCH. No they flaming well ain't! Not if I can help it!

> **DEBBIE** *shouts up again. The Felsworth characters freeze.*

DEBBIE. What time's the babysitter coming?

> **CHRIS** *mouths 'shit' – he hasn't arranged a babysitter!*

CHRIS. Oh, erm… seven? Ish?

DEBBIE. Okay, long as she's not late. Are you getting ready?

CHRIS. Yeah yeah.

> *And he's back to the comic. All the Felsworth folk come alive once more.*

JACKIE. Titch, what are you going to do? Felsworth International Bank is on the 48th floor of state-of-the-art skyscraper Felsworth Towers!

TITCH. If I can break through the defence of the crack Movaranian league champions – twice – to win that

charity match behind the flippin iron curtain –
I reckon I can break into anywhere!

JACKIE. Oh, Titch, what if you're killed and I never see you
again!

TITCH. Not bloomin' likely! Not when we're playing
Fishtown City tomorrow!

SELBY. Always a slippery outfit!

JACKIE. I just don't know what I'd do without you! I love
you, Titch McCreavie! I love you!!

She smiles lovingly and they kiss. **CHRIS** *closes his eyes
and dreams.* **DEBBIE***'s voice cuts through – all freeze.*

DEBBIE. Chris, are you still sat on your arse up there? And
have you ordered a taxi? You better have.

CHRIS. *(absent-mindedly)* Yeah, I'm on it, stay calm.

There are rolls of thunder in the distance.

SELBY. Quick, get those spare goal nets from my car, Flame-
haired Speedster!

TITCH. Great thinking, boss! I'll be able to wrap those
armed robbers up in the old onion bag!

SELBY. It'll be the best hat-trick you ever score, Titch!

TITCH. And Jackie, book us a table at Luigi's Ristorante for
tonight – saving the day always makes me hungry!

JACKIE. Of course, darling.

DEBBIE. *(offstage)* Simon's expecting us at eight!

DEBBIE *enters the attic.*

DEBBIE. What are you doing? Have you rung the babysitter?

CHRIS. Who? What? Erm, yep, just coming.

DEBBIE. You're not changed. You haven't even moved.

DEBBIE *twigs.*

Or sorted out the sitter. Have you?

CHRIS. Erm, about the sitter… we may not need one.

*CHRIS looks at the comic. **DEBBIE** snatches it from him. Big thunder and lightning. The Felsworth characters exit under **SELBY**'s brolly.*

DEBBIE. Why not?

CHRIS. Look, Debbie, I don't want a big row…

DEBBIE. Tough luck, 'cos you're about to get one!

CHRIS. I just… don't want to go.

DEBBIE. So what? You want me to go on my own, is that it?

CHRIS. He's your boss. You *like* him.

DEBBIE. And you're my husband.

CHRIS. He winds me up!

DEBBIE. You wind *me* up.

CHRIS. Then you know what I mean don't you?

DEBBIE. No! I don't actually! You used to make me laugh, and light me up inside. Now half the time I want to bloody throttle you.

CHRIS. And the other half?

DEBBIE. Run you over!

CHRIS. Is that really how you feel?

DEBBIE. Don't you? We never smile anymore.

CHRIS. I smiled last month. I was faking it, though.

DEBBIE. I thought kids were supposed to keep couples together.

CHRIS. Here we go.

DEBBIE. Well, do you see a future? As it is? Because I bloody don't!

CHRIS. Oh, well, listen; let's not *work* at it or anything!

DEBBIE. You!? Work?

CHRIS. There you go again, in for the kill! Count Otto Von Gorschnitz has nothing on you, has he?

DEBBIE. Oh sod off, then!

CHRIS. Tell you what, go for Christmas drinks at Simon's if that's what you want, but don't ask me to come. Enjoy. Bye bye!

DEBBIE. Fine… Thanks for the support. Much appreciated.

She throws the comic at him and exits. **CHRIS** *picks it up and looks at it.* **TITCH** *enters, with a bundle in his arms. More thunder. He sinks to his knees.*

TITCH. Well, that's those armed robbers tied up and left for Felsworth Constabulary to get them under lock and key… but damn that stray bullet! If I can't save this baby's life, all my efforts at the bank will have been for nothing!

He reaches inside his tracksuit for his lucky locket.

Whiskers, I'm asking you… help me… help me save this child…

The thunder and lightning gets louder and louder. **CHRIS** *is idly fiddling with the locket as he reads the comic.*

I'm no doctor, kid, but I'll be damned if I'm going to let you miss Christmas! I just have to remember the medical training they gave me when I was a nipper in the orphanage! But for now…

He puts the locket round the bundle. More thunder and lightning. **DEBBIE** *shouts from below.*

DEBBIE. *(off)* Right I'm going! Bye!

CHRIS. *(shouting off)* Bloody bye!

TITCH. Come on, kid… pull through… please!

DEBBIE. *(off)* Fine.

CHRIS. *(shouting off)* Fine!

TITCH. Do it for me!

DEBBIE. *(off)* Don't bother to wait up!

TITCH. For the orphans!

CHRIS. *(shouting off)* I won't!

DEBBIE. *(off)* Good!

CHRIS. *(shouts)* Cracking!

Thunder. Lightning. **TITCH** *is rubbing the locket round the baby's neck.* **CHRIS** *is feverishly doing the same.*

TITCH. But most of all…

DEBBIE. *(off)* Go live in the past! I hope you and Titch are happy!

TITCH. Most of all…

CHRIS. *(shouting off)* What?

DEBBIE. *(off)* Sod off to Felswick!

CHRIS. *(shouting off)* For the last time…

TITCH. Do it…

> *Thunder and lightning. The next two lines are spoken over one another, so that* **TITCH** *and* **CHRIS** *say 'Felsworth' at the same moment.*

TITCH. … for FELSWORTH!

CHRIS. … it's FELSWORTH!

> *Now the thunder and lightning is ramped up to full tilt. The music comes in full blast.* **CHRIS** *is almost thrown out of his seat with the force of the moment.* **TITCH MCCREAVIE** *and* **CHRIS** *remain – they hold an identical pose as the locket suddenly transports them both back to 1978. Suddenly all is silence and stillness.*

Scene Five

> *Lights change. We are back in the bedroom of* **CHRIS**'s *imagination. Or are we?* **JULIE** *calls from off stage again.)*

JULIE. *(off)* Christopher!

> **CHRIS** *rubs his face, like he is recovering from the worst piss-up in history. Enter* **JULIE**, *but* **CHRIS** *doesn't recognise her – he assumes it's* **DEBBIE** *back to harangue him again.*

JULIE. Christopher!

CHRIS. For the last damn time, I am not going, okay!?

JULIE. I'll give you not going! Now put the flaming comics away and get ready for school!

> **CHRIS** *looks up sharply – that's not* **DEBBIE***! He sees his mum now and nearly jumps out of the chair.*

CHRIS. Mother!?… Mum?

JULIE. No, the cat's Auntie Margaret! Who else?

> **CHRIS** *is baffled. Is he dreaming, drunk, both?*

JULIE. Come on, comic down, look at the time! *(pause)* What's the matter with you?

CHRIS. *(pause)* Mum?

JULIE. Yes! Me, Mum… you, Christopher… I give up! You're going to be late. Again!

CHRIS. Late?

JULIE. *(apeing* **CHRIS**'s *face)* That's right. Now get dressed!

CHRIS. Dressed?

JULIE. Is there an echo in here? Come on, your games kit is in your bag.

CHRIS. Games?

JULIE. Yes. What is wrong with you this morning?

CHRIS. Morning? I must have drunk more than I thought…

JULIE. Drunk? If you've been stealing your dad's Bacardi.

CHRIS. Mum, no, I haven't done that since I was…

> *A beat. There is a hint of music, and a very distant rumble of thunder low in the mix.* **CHRIS** *looks at the locket round his neck. Something very serious has happened.*

Oh shit.

JULIE. I'll pretend you didn't say that.

CHRIS. This is… really weird… Mum?! Is it *you?*

JULIE. Now get downstairs! Your dad might give you a lift but don't go on about that trip again because between you and me…

CHRIS. What trip?

JULIE. Er, the one you've been going on about for months? To Bruges?

CHRIS. Bruges…? Bruges? Oh my God. It's 1978?!

JULIE. Christopher will you stop mucking about! Now come on, two more days and school breaks up for Christmas.

CHRIS. School?

JULIE. What's up? Are you sick?

CHRIS. Yeah… I'm just not sure what of. No, I'm…listen to me carefully… I don't know what this is, maybe I'm hallucinating, but… Mum, I'm a fully grown man and I am not going to school.

JULIE. What are you talking about? You're thirteen!

CHRIS. I'm what?

JULIE. Look…is this about what I caught you doing?

CHRIS. Eh?

JULIE. Because it's nothing to be embarrassed about…

CHRIS. What isn't? *(remembers – recoils)* Oh! God, no! Jesus! You should have knocked; it were your own fault. I'd forgot about that!

JULIE. I'm only saying. Now, you are a man, you're my little man, always, alright. I just want you to… be like other lads. Happy. Now you *have* remembered about your grandad, haven't you?

CHRIS. *(cautiously)* What…?

JULIE. Having your room. Only he's got here a bit early, and—

CHRIS. Grandad? He's here? Now?

JULIE. He's downstairs, and I think he could do with a lie-down, so—

CHRIS. Oh my – I've got to – bloody hell!

He grabs his uniform out of the laundry basket and dashes offstage.

JULIE. Your blazer's hanging on the back of the…

But he's gone. She rolls her eyes and exits momentarily.

Scene Six

Music. Lights. **CHRIS** *exits. The stage is reconfigured by* **JULIE** *and* **GRANDAD**, *chairs being brought more tightly into a central space, standard lamps moving and so on. A Christmas tree has also appeared. At the conclusion of the change,* **GRANDAD** *sits in the chair, wheezing.* **JULIE** *is looking for her husband.*

JULIE. Where's Ian?

GRANDAD. Gone.

JULIE. He could have bloody – I told Christopher he'd give him a lift!

GRANDAD. Too late. Like looking for the bloody Invisible Man half the time anyway.

JULIE. Don't start, Ian has a lot on at the moment.

GRANDAD. Only saying. Christopher awake?

JULIE. Yeah. He had his face buried in his silly comics when I went in.

GRANDAD. Good of him to let me have his bedroom.

JULIE. Oh, he's a good lad really. Said he wasn't going to school, but—

GRANDAD. Is he badly?

JULIE. No, just away with the Flame-haired Dynamo or in dream land somewhere, as ever, only more than usual this morning... I think that other boy he's had the trouble with... Dewhirst...might be what's putting him off.

GRANDAD. 'Appen. I only learned one thing in school. Keep your head down, mouth shut, never take your eye off your dinner, never put your hand up first and if the teacher says 'Just tell the truth; I won't be angry,' never, ever bloody fall for it.

JULIE. Pity you didn't learn to count, that's about six things, Dad.

Enter **CHRIS**. *He is in a school suit, jacket and trousers both way too short.* **JULIE** *and* **GRANDAD** *both look at* *him like he looks really smart.* **CHRIS** *stops dead on sight of his* **GRANDAD**. *Neither speaks.* **GRANDAD** *is looking up and down his shirt or to see if his flies are undone.*

CHRIS. Grandad...?

GRANDAD. Aye... hello lad.

The old boy looks at him and winks. **CHRIS** *walks to him, and hugs him. He holds the old boy for a long moment. He is on the point of tears.*

CHRIS. Hello, mate.

GRANDAD. I thought you'd be hoppin' mad, having to give your bedroom up for an old git like me.

CHRIS. No worries, easy come easy go. Good to see you again.

GRANDAD. It's only been a week.

CHRIS. Yeah. Just er... feels longer.

JULIE. Your dad's done another disappearing act, so you're walking to school.

CHRIS. Erm... about the er... the uniform here, Mum... think we need to...

JULIE. Starting to fit you nice, that jacket now. I said we needed to get a size bigger...

CHRIS. What!?

DEB. So you'd grow into it.

CHRIS. Mum, are you blind? Grandad, tell her.

DEB. Would he listen? No, would he, heck, what do I know? I'm daft, I'm stupid, now look at him. Bobby Dazzler!

GRANDAD. It is a bit big on him.

CHRIS. Big?!

GRANDAD. You'll look like James Bond when it fits you proper, mind.

CHRIS. What, after Blofeld boil washed him for a week!?

GRANDAD. You're the smartest fella in class, I'll bet.

JULIE. Not according to his report.

CHRIS. Or his tailor! Come on! You can't see this?

JULIE. I loved school. Wish I'd done more... had half the chances you have, to go to university, travel...

CHRIS. Listen, it's been a cracker to see you all, but I probably should be going... I mean... going. Waking up!

CHRIS slaps himself in the face.

Come on. Come on.

JULIE. ...instead of always a big long list of what I couldn't do.

CHRIS. You say that... *(slaps himself)* ... but maybe it would have only confused things. *(slaps himself)* Plus, you wouldn't have married dad or had me!

JULIE. Don't rub it in. And get to school.

CHRIS. I really, really can't.

JULIE. And ask if there's anything Fiona doesn't like.

CHRIS. Eh?

JULIE. For tea! You insisted on inviting her and it's this evening!

CHRIS. Oh, er... course it is.

JULIE. Thing is, they eat different stuff, don't they... her type...

CHRIS. Girls?

GRANDAD. Southerners.

JULIE. People from London, I mean, oh don't say she's vegetarian because your dad won't have that in the house... broccoli and green cauliflower, people who don't eat bacon and whatever else.

CHRIS. Mum, far as I know broccoli is not part of a London conspiracy to skewer the north.

JULIE. Because I want to do your favourite.

CHRIS suddenly grins, ear to ear, he'd forgotten this.

CHRIS. Spam fritters!

JULIE. Chips and beans!

CHRIS. Bread and marg!

JULIE. And for pudding?

CHRIS. Angel Delight!

GRANDAD. And a bottle of brown ale!

CHRIS. Or three! Amen, Grandad. That'll do fine mum.

JULIE. She's lovely this Fiona, I met her at the carol concert, and talented, she plays the violin.

GRANDAD. What the hell's she bothering with him for, then?

CHRIS. Good question. What carol concert?

JULIE. I'm going to have you to the doctor, the one you, me and Auntie Margaret were at last week!

CHRIS. Oh right, yeah, course, *that* carol concert. Now I remember. Yeah, it were good.

JULIE. Right taken with her, I was, and I didn't expect to be, with her family being… you know… what they are…?

CHRIS. *(after a pause)* They were socialists, Mum, not head-hunting cannibals.

JULIE. Well your dad says it's weird anyway. Oh, you do look handsome. I don't know, kid – one minute you're that age, and the next… you're me.

CHRIS. How old are you?

JULIE. Old. I'm thirty-three.

He grins at her.

CHRIS. Thirty-three…? Is that all? Bloody hell.

JULIE. You won't be saying that when you're this age, believe me. Now skidaddle! 'Appen Fiona will get some sense out of you.

Music. The stage is reconfigured.

Scene Seven

Enter **FIONA**, *playing her violin.* **CHRIS** *joins her. They are in the background, before the start of school. He stares at her a moment.*

CHRIS. Fiona... Fiona Garbutt...how weird is this?

He goes to hug her, to her surprise. She backs off.

FIONA. Er Christopher McCann!

CHRIS. Sorry... sorry... bit much... *(he looks at her, smiling)* I was right.

FIONA. What about?

CHRIS. You. In every way. Wow... you sound the same, look even prettier... in every detail...

FIONA. What are you on about?

CHRIS. Than I remember you.

FIONA. You only saw me yesterday!

CHRIS. I did...? And... I didn't... I don't mean to freak you out but, I need help, right, and you're pretty much the only person I think will believe me.

FIONA. Let me guess, you haven't done your homework? Again!

CHRIS. What? Oh shit, there's that as well.

FIONA does palm to forehead, shaking of head.

FIONA. Oh what will become of this youth?

CHRIS. I could tell you, but you'll weep. Listen...

FIONA. You can copy mine if...

CHRIS. If?

FIONA. Instead of coming for tea – you do know I'm vegetarian, don't you?

CHRIS. Oh shit! Are you? I don't remember that.

FIONA. Leave it. I can come later and we watch the documentary about Kate Bush on BBC2.

CHRIS. Kate Bush? Oh my God... I remember it. Thing is, we weren't a BBC 2 family, Fiona.

FIONA. Until you met me! Well it's my way – or the homework detention highway, Christopher McCann. You decide!

CHRIS. Look, can't we just twag school, and watch Kate Bush at yours instead?

FIONA. We don't have a television.

CHRIS. Course, I'd forgotten that.

FIONA. Dad says it's just a diet of right wing propaganda and sexist stereotypes.

CHRIS. Does he? My old man couldn't even spell that.

FIONA. Please take care not to copy the English *too* slavishly as the teacher will recognize some of my finer stylistic flourishes.

> **CHRIS** *commences copying.* **DEWHIRST** *enters, a mean-looking bully type.*

FIONA. Ah. It's that dreadful cad Dewhirst, your bête noir. He of Grimy Shirt Collar Close and Mucky Fingernail Paddock. He seems most anxious to knock your block off by the way.

CHRIS. Fiona we're not in *Pride and Prejudice* now!

FIONA. What a book! Shall we go another way?

DEWHIRST. You avoiding me, McCann?

> *Enter* **CRADDOCK** *in full dramatic guns a-blazing style.*

CRADDOCK. Achtung achtung, Gott im Himmel, Dewhirst at 9 o'clock! Christopher… you know what to do, son.

CHRIS. Yeah… run like the clappers!

CRADDOCK. What the blazes!? You ain't scared of him, are you?

CHRIS. Yes. Okay, here we go, smack in the gob time.

DEWHIRST. McCann. You owe me a Curly Wurly.

CHRIS. A Curly W – all this over a Curly Wurly…?

DEWHIRST. You got one?

CHRIS. *(wincing)* No…?

DEWHIRST *grabs* CHRIS. *He is winding up to give him a walloping.* CHRIS *says the first thing that comes into his head in a blind panic.*

I don't buy them, my grandad says you're paying for holes!

A moment. DEWHIRST *thinks on this for a second.*

DEWHIRST. I like the holes best!

FIONA. What!?

CHRIS. See what I'm up against? And he ends up a manager at B&Q and I'm unemployed, how can that be right!?

DEWHIRST. One Curly Wurly by end of school – or it's end of you! Okay?

He releases CHRIS, *and exits.*

See you later.

CHRIS. Yeah, that's fine mate, crackin'! No worries. You braindead div! What's the betting he'll chuck me in the canal later, for a laugh, you know.

FIONA. Really?

CHRIS. Sadly. Oh my God, school, is this happening? Mr Reynolds the science teacher lights a fag in class, scratches his backside, says – 'there's only three things you need to know about science. If it stinks it's chemistry, if it's dead it's biology and if it don't bloody work it's physics! Dewhirst, don't dangle McCann out of the window like that, lad, get him by both ankles!'

FIONA. You're funny.

CHRIS. Sometimes. I used to be.

He smiles ruefully. FIONA *grins at him.*

FIONA. I'm glad we live on your street. It's as though we were fated to meet and become lifelong friends!

CHRIS. You won't say that when I'm sick all over you at the pictures.

FIONA. You're also strange, Christopher McCann. More than usual, even.

CHRIS. Yeah. Now about that—

The bell rings for school.

FIONA. No time; il faut que je m'en aille!

CHRIS. What?

FIONA. French first period! Got to go! À bientôt, Christophe!

CHRIS. What?

FIONA. No! Qu'est-ce que c'est? Later alligator!

She dashes off. Music. Probably some Kate Bush. The living room is recreated.

CHRIS. If you say so. All these years later…and she still ties me up in knots…how weird is this?

Scene Eight

Enter **IAN**. *He is in a white shirt, tie, he has a briefcase, every inch the businessman.*

GRANDAD *is sat in the chair wheezing as ever, and* **JULIE** *is upstage with an apron on.*

IAN. Evening all. How's the patient?

GRANDAD. Sick as a box of frogs. Bugger off.

IAN. Charming as ever. Where's Christopher?

JULIE. In his room.

IAN. What's he doing? He's not…*(nods; winks)* again, is he?

JULIE. No, and don't tell him I told you that! He wouldn't go to school. Set off, then came home. He's been sitting in the middle of the room, with that bloody plastic necklace on, shouting 'home!' and 'Felsworth!' at the top of his voice.

GRANDAD. Lad's gone crackers if you ask me.

IAN. I didn't. I'm not having this. First the report, now this? *(shouts)* Christopher! Has he been knocking about with the strange girl again?

JULIE. Her name's Fiona, and she's very nice. In fact… he's invited her for tea, so behave yourself.

Enter **CHRIS**, *the locket round his neck and a pile of comics under one arm.*

CHRIS. Eh up, Dad. How you doing, feller?

IAN. *(taken aback)* Er, don't you dare 'eh up feller' *me*, young feller, what's this I hear about you bunking off, eh up feller oh aye?

CHRIS. It's pointless me trying to explain it.

IAN. No it's not. Well?

CHRIS. Well what?

IAN. Is going on? You're behaving very strangely. This girl... Fiona... her parents... you can tell us... have there been any... bizarre *rituals*?

CHRIS. *(after a pause)* Dad they're socialists not satanists.

IAN. Thin line! Then what's going on? You're reading too many comics! The country's gone to the dogs, it's time to stop reading, son, and start *doing. Doing, doing doing*!

CHRIS. That's what I've been trying to do all day. I've been trying to go home, but it's not working.

IAN. Home? You are home. *(pause)* Is it glue, son?

CHRIS. What?

JULIE. Ian!

IAN. It's a fair question. It took him a month to make that Triceratops, and it only had three pieces.

CHRIS. It was faulty!

GRANDAD. I did it in five minutes.

IAN. Well? Is it?

CHRIS. I am not sniffing glue. Bloody hellfire!

GRANDAD. I might start in a minute.

IAN. Good. Now sit up straight, fasten your tie properly, makes an important statement about who you are, what you believe in.

CHRIS. Does it?

IAN. Out there, at the sharp end, cutting a deal, a bit of pride in your appearance separates the glue sniffers from such as me – those who take charge of their own destiny. We've got to be doers, not waiters.

GRANDAD. At least waiters earn tips.

JULIE. Dad.

IAN. These are dark days. Strikes, walkouts, unions. The Russians must be laughing all the way to the gulags! Bloody Labour government destroying the country!

GRANDAD *breaks into hacking coughs.*

JULIE. Dad!

JULIE goes to **GRANDAD**. **IAN** *beckons* **CHRIS** *over to him, speaks conspiratorially.*

IAN. Now... quiet word, Christopher. Your birthday the other week... did you have a good day out? That Flamingo Land, some place eh?

CHRIS. Yeah. Would have been better to see it from the inside, Dad, but what the heck eh?

IAN. Good point, accepted. Bit dearer than I thought, you know, couple of cheques didn't come through in time. Next time, you are going in for sure! Now not a word to your mum, but, erm, your birthday money? Don't still have a couple of quid left do you? Fiver say?

CHRIS. What!?

CHRIS pauses, looks at him blankly.

CHRIS. You borrowed my birthday money back off me... I forgot about this.

IAN. Just till Monday and a cheque clears, big one at that. You'll get it back and more, a tenner, it's yours. Done?

CHRIS. *(thinks)* Where to start... In my tin, on the bedroom windowsill.

IAN. Monday, you're getting a tenner back.

CHRIS. *(after a pause)* Don't worry about it.

There is a knock at the door. **JULIE** *goes to answer it and returns with* **FIONA**.

IAN. Of course I worry about it. This is your father speaking, you are getting a tenner back. Yes. Start thinking what to spend it on, because it's yours already. Money is merely a tool, Christopher, a lever. It's knowing how to use it… control it. You'll learn.

CHRIS. Oh I will. Just too bloody late.

IAN exits to get the fiver. CHRIS goes to his GRANDAD.

How you feeling, Grandad?

GRANDAD. Like shit. Gagging for a fag. Mind, Citizen Smith starts in a bit. At least there's that.

CHRIS. Ah, now, thing is I promised my… I promised Fiona we could watch the Kate Bush thing on BBC2.

GRANDAD. Who the hell's Kate Bush?

JULIE returns with FIONA.

JULIE. Look who's here.

FIONA. Hello.

JULIE. Christopher? Are you going to put them comics away now, love? Your friend's here.

CHRIS starts looking through the comics. IAN retuns.

CHRIS. There has to be something in here…

IAN. This is Fiona, is it? Well you're very welcome to join us for a McCann family evening.

FIONA. Thank you.

IAN nonchalantly pulls the fiver out of his pocket, holds it up.

IAN. Why I feel that liebfraumilch moment approaching! Blue Nun, Chateau '77, excellent vintage.

JULIE. Smashing idea! Sit you down, sweetheart, look like you're stopping. Would you like a biscuit?

FIONA. No, thank you.

JULIE. A piece of cake?

FIONA. No, really, it's fine.

JULIE. An apple?

FIONA. I'm fine,

JULIE. Orange?

FIONA. I couldn't…

JULIE. Jaffa cake?

FIONA. Honestly.

JULIE. Are you sure?

FIONA. Quite.

JULIE. A drink then? Christopher, get Fiona some orange squash.

CHRIS. Mum, she isn't bothered.

JULIE. Oh there's some cream soda!

FIONA. No, really.

JULIE. It's no bother.

CHRIS. Mum, don't worry about it.

JULIE. Tea, coffee?

CHRIS. *(finally)* Oh Jesus Christ!

GRANDAD. Was born in Bethlehem!

CHRIS. She don't want anything and don't start the same rigmarole now over a bloody cardigan. She's warm enough as well!

JULIE. Alright, mardy pants!

GRANDAD. Is he goin to't shop? I'll have twenty Bensons.

JULIE. You will not.

FIONA. Is it always like this?

CHRIS. Sadly.

JULIE. Christopher, for the last time! Comics! Away! *(to FIONA)* So sorry, love, he invites you over…

GRANDAD. Takes over the telly!

FIONA. Yes, thank you for this, it's lovely. We don't have one in our house.

JULIE. *(after a pause)* You what?

FIONA. We don't have a telly.

JULIE. Oh my God! Aw, sweetheart, I am sorry, you can come here anytime, darling. Are you sure you're not hungry, do you need a bath?

CHRIS. Mother, she's fine, she's just come to watch Kate Bush!

JULIE. Well, you're very welcome. I'm sorry, children going without upsets me, and at Christmas as well I...

IAN. We have a new colour set as you can see, Fiona.

GRANDAD. It's only rented.

JULIE. And the feller were knocking on the door for the money yesterday and I'd to hide behind the flaming settee.

IAN coughs and glares at JULIE *to keep quiet on that in front of* FIONA.

JULIE. Again.

FIONA. My dad won't have a television in the house.

IAN. Doesn't he work, your father?

FIONA. Yes, he's an English teacher and folklorist.

IAN. Very good. Julie loves flowers, so—

JULIE. *Folklorist...* not florist! So, have you really never seen Blankety Blank?

FIONA. Never.

IAN. Charlie's Angels?

FIONA. No.

IAN. Excellent programme.

CHRIS. Someone shoot me. Please.

JULIE. Is this it starting now?

All but CHRIS *sit for a moment looking out at the TV. CHRIS still has his head in the comics. We hear the opening strains of 'Wuthering Heights'.*

GRANDAD. Kate Bush? It isn't her doing gymnastics wailing about bloody Heathcliff is it?

FIONA. She's amazing. *Wuthering Heights* is actually a novel, by Emily Brontë.

JULIE. Oh is it a book as well? I remember the film.

FIONA. I want to be a writer.

JULIE. Oh, smashing.

FIONA. Or a singer.

JULIE. No!

FIONA. Or possibly a clothes designer.

JULIE. Go away?

FIONA. Or all of the above.

JULIE. You will be.

FIONA. How do you know?

JULIE. I can just tell. Same as I knew when I were twelve. I looked at myself in the mirror and said... teenage bride, hairdresser, but above all... smoker.

IAN. *Wuthering Heights?*

FIONA. It's about a girl, Cathy, and she lives at Wuthering Heights.

GRANDAD. At Haworth. Near Bradford.

FIONA. Imagine a wild, rugged, windswept, tempestuous and deeply desolate place.

GRANDAD. I don't have to, I've been to Bradford.

FIONA. Cathy and Heathcliff are two innocent children thrown together... in a cruel and unforgiving place. It's amazing!

JULIE. I remember the film were miserable. Don't she die?

GRANDAD. *(at telly)* Does she know that frock's see through?

JULIE. I think she does, Dad, alright, calm down.

GRANDAD. *(at telly)* What's she doing with her arms? Looks like she's having a bloody seizure.

JULIE. Dad!

GRANDAD. I'm missing Citizen Smith for this.

FIONA. Are you coming to Bruges, Christopher? I can't wait. Say you'll come; it's only £65.

CHRIS *looks up from the comics.*

IAN. *(gulps)* £65!? What's the trip for?

FIONA. To look at the art and culture.

JULIE. Oh I don't care for all that. I'd sooner we got a new sofa.

GRANDAD. Or paid for the telly.

IAN. £65. No problem, and do you know why?

CHRIS. Because Fiona's here and you can't stand to look cheap.

IAN. My father, Fiona, he worked every day of his life, he never put his hands on £65 at one go. He lived and died in a council house.

JULIE. *(after a pause)* We live in a council house.

IAN. Now we do! Now, yes, but it is the council estate of the mind we must escape.

JULIE. Oh for—

IAN. It cannot hold us... do you see?

All slowly shake their heads.

I want you to *dream*, Christopher... that's what I'm saying to you... I want you to *dare*. Go to Bruges...

CHRIS. I'd forgotten you used to come out with all this.

GRANDAD. Am I the only bugger watching this?

JULIE. What are you doing for Christmas, Fiona love? Have you got family coming?

FIONA. No. Dad wants to spend the time preparing for the revolution, so...

CHRIS *is suddenly on high alert.*

IAN. What revolution?

CHRIS. Easy now.

FIONA. The one that's just around the corner! Mum and Dad reckon the socialist dawn is on the horizon. Don't you watch the news?!

IAN. No, and neither do you, you haven't got a telly.

FIONA. The 80s will be the decade when the workers strike the killer blow to this morally bankrupt system! You must be really excited about it too?

JULIE. I am, sweetheart, but I want to get Christmas out of the way first.

FIONA. Mr McCann, surely you're a socialist?

All cough, gasp at that.

CHRIS. Oh dear. Here we go…

IAN. I beg your cardigan?

FIONA. A socialist. You are working class, after all.

IAN. *(appalled)* Working class?

CHRIS. … and they're off.

IAN. Young lady you are a guest in this house and I will thank you not to cast *aspersions.* I am of the business and entrepreneurial class; do you know what that means?

JULIE. It means *I* work every hour God sends to keep this house while he's out 'til all hours '*chasing dreams*', love.

IAN. Look at me – I go to work in a suit. Do you think a member of the working class would wear a suit like this?

GRANDAD. No one should wear a suit like that.

FIONA. Well…

CHRIS. *(to himself)* Please, this time – just leave it…

FIONA. … my dad thinks that it's everyone's right to a fair and equal system! That's what the revolution will be about!

CHRIS. *(to himself)* I can't even drink.

IAN. You have a great deal to learn about the world, young lady!

GRANDAD. Listen who's talking.

IAN. Mrs Thatcher…

FIONA. She's the enemy!

IAN. She's the best man in Britain.

CHRIS. *(under his breath)* Ding, dong, the witch is dead…

JULIE. Ooh, is *The Wizard of Oz* on?

GRANDAD. Be a change if it's not.

JULIE. *Sound Of Music,* that's my favourite.

IAN. She'll sort out the unions!

GRANDAD. Who, Julie Andrews?

IAN. Maggie!

FIONA. She'll destroy this country and the working class with it!

IAN. Rubbish!

FIONA. Dad says!

IAN. Rubbish!

CHRIS. All right, enough! How's about I just cut to the chase, 'cos I aren't sitting through this again. You *(to FIONA)* get upset, which means Mum turns on you *(to IAN)* and tells Fiona not to end up like her.

JULIE. *(weeping)* Straight from school to a maternity frock...

CHRIS. You don't apologise, so Grandad wades in, which sets him off coughing, you get the monk on; Fiona, you sit on the step and cry...

JULIE. I've done it plenty of times, love.

CHRIS. Then there's more rowing about the Heath government and the three-day week – somehow the Watney cup gets brought into it, you *(to FIONA)* tip a cup of squash on Dad, Grandad wets himself laughing, the neighbours bang on the wall and you end up banned from our house. Everyone happy? Good. Come on, Fiona.

> **CHRIS** *takes* **FIONA** *by the hand and they exit. No one speaks for a second.*

GRANDAD. Now can I watch *Citizen Smith*? I've bloody missed it haven't I?

> *Music. The stage is reconfigured.*

Scene Nine

CHRIS *and* FIONA *enter. Sit together.*

FIONA. Erm… sorry… think I might have…

CHRIS. Not your fault at all. Wow… that has just… done my head…

FIONA. Are you okay?

CHRIS. Yeah. Well, no, but… When I were a kid I worshipped the ground he walked on, and all he did was… sorry about… you know… and don't worry about the ban – your mum brings some home brew round on Christmas Eve, and it's all sins forgiven, but then I get walloped on it before new year. What's in it by the way?

FIONA. Wow… it's nettle wine… Mum just said today that she'll take some round… on Christmas Eve… How do you know that?

CHRIS. Right – we're alone, aren't we?

They both look round. No one about.

I'm warning you, this is going to sound mental.

FIONA. Don't worry, I already think you're mental.

CHRIS. Okay. Here goes… I'm a middle-aged man. From the future.

FIONA. *(after a pause)* Sorry?

CHRIS. Yeah.

FIONA. Right. That is a *bit* mental.

CHRIS. I know, but it's true.

FIONA. Christopher… I understand.

CHRIS. You do?! Bless you… you're the only one I could tell…

FIONA. I live half in the real world and half in fantasy land too.

CHRIS. What?

FIONA. One day I'm Elizabeth Bennett from *Pride and Prejudice* and the next Cathy from *Wuthering Heights*…

CHRIS. No no no! I'm not dreaming it! It's real. Okay... if you want proof... erm... aha! I know what you've got me for Christmas.

FIONA. Go on?

CHRIS. *The Mayor of Casterbridge.*

> **FIONA** *does a sharp intake of breath.*

Right?

> **FIONA** *nods dumbly.*

And on the inside cover you've written, 'To Mr. Christopher McCann, my best new friend. Merry Christmas and a Socialist New Year. Kiss-kiss.'

FIONA. What!? How can you know that!? I only just wrote that today. Spent all afternoon agonising... one kiss or two... what will he think?

CHRIS. Two's fine. Three would have been forward, but two is good... Believe me, I remember I read that card, and looked at those kisses, more than I did these comics.

FIONA. Is this... *real?*

CHRIS. Yeah. It is. Now... don't run away or scream or anything. I'm not here to, you know, steal your mind or... whatever...

> **FIONA** *looks* **CHRIS** *up and down.*

FIONA. No. Okay. Okay. Wow. I mean... like really... wow! Either you're just like my Uncle Clive—

CHRIS. What!? You mean there's more of us? He's from the future too?

FIONA. No he's just dangerously insane. He spent 1974 convinced he was an emperor penguin. He's heavily medicated, it's very sad. Or... you're telling the truth.

CHRIS. Fiona...

FIONA. What?

CHRIS. *(eye contact)* I know I'm not a penguin.

FIONA. *(pause)* Oh my... So when are you from?

CHRIS. 2013.

FIONA. Which means you're—

CHRIS. Don't say it out loud, it'll only depress me.

FIONA. And why did you come here?

CHRIS. I've no idea. Or how I got here. I was holding onto this locket – well, it's a replica, and there was this storm, and—

CHRIS gets comics out of his bag. Starts passing some over to FIONA.

I know it's got something to do with Titch McCreavie, I just can't work out what it is. But... he was there, when I... I saw him, I think, when...

FIONA has found the Christmas card.

FIONA. 'Merry Christmas, Fiona.' No kiss. Okay. Fine.

CHRIS. I used to be shy.

FIONA. 'PS. Please will you come to the pictures with me in the holidays to watch *Jaws 2* at the Odeon.' Why on earth would I want to see *Jaws 2?*

CHRIS. What? Erm, maybe 'cos it's got a shark in it!?

FIONA. Not a huge enticement.

CHRIS. I disagree.

FIONA. Speaks volumes.

CHRIS. Two of the finest films ever made, the third one's a bit—

FIONA. Christopher McCann! We need to think... this Titch McCreavie – tell me about him. Why is he known as the Flame-haired Dynamo?

CHRIS. Because he's got flaming red hair. Plus, he carries a lock of red hair in a locket around his neck, just like this one.

He proudly shows her the locket he's wearing.

He never takes it off. It belonged to his only known relative, Whiskers McCreavie, who's long-since dead but visits him from beyond the grave to offer words of wisdom in times of crisis.

FIONA. And who's this?

CHRIS. That's Jackie, she's his girlfriend.

FIONA. What does she do, apart from stand about saying 'I love you, Titch' all the time?

CHRIS. She's a secretary at Felsworth Bank, on the 48th floor of state-of-the-art skyscraper Felsworth Towers in the heart of Felsworth's thriving technology quarter.

FIONA. *(not listening)* What a load of rubbish.

CHRIS. Oh, not you as well.

> **FIONA** *is now drawn into the comics.*

FIONA. Look at how she's drawn. All she does is simper, and look up over her huge eyelashes. A secretary? Because she couldn't possibly be the boss herself, could she?

CHRIS. Well… the story's not about her, is it…?

FIONA. Wouldn't be, would it!?

CHRIS. It's a boys' comic! Bloody hell!

FIONA. I shall have no male boss so long as I live.

CHRIS. I believe you. Can we get back to—

FIONA. Look… every time she appears. 'I love you, Titch! I love you, Titch!' Why can't she have anything else to say? 'Oh, Titch, you've saved us again!' Sorry, my opinion stands.

CHRIS. Which is—?

FIONA. That the Brontës, Dickens, Jane Austen and so on is serious literature, whilst comics are just stupid, vapid, sexist drivel…

CHRIS. They're not stupid! They're the literature of the common man.

FIONA. Yes, if the common man is a moron!

> **DEWHIRST** *enters.*

DEWHIRST. McCann!

FIONA. Ah. Perfect timing!

CHRIS. Shit. OK, point to you.

DEWHIRST. You owe me a Curly Wurly.

He snatches the comic from **CHRIS**.

What's this? Puff Weekly?

Enter **CRADDOCK**, *tunic open, blood on his vest. Bandage on his head.*

CRADDOCK. Free at last! Over that ridge, and the nightmare is over.

FIONA. Do you want to give it back?

DEWHIRST. *(imitating* **FIONA**) 'Do you want to give it back?' Not really.

FIONA. Why don't you leave him alone?

DEWHIRST. Look at this, McCann – a girl to fight your battles for you.

FIONA. Come on, Christopher, let's just go…

DEWHIRST. Yeah, *(imitating* **FIONA**) 'Come on, Christopher…'

CRADDOCK. Count Otto, I've been tortured by you long enough!

FIONA. Get lost, Dewhirst. You don't scare me, you big bully!

DEWHIRST. No?

FIONA. NO!

DEWHIRST. NO…?

CHRIS. *(yelling)* THAT'S IT!

DEWHIRST. What's it?

CHRIS. I've been tortured by you long enough!

DEWHIRST. No you haven't, I'm not bored of it at all yet.

CHRIS. Maybe I should run, but I'm staying right here.

FIONA. No you should definitely run!

CRADDOCK. You're going to get what's coming to you! You Nazi stooge!

CHRIS. You're going to get what's coming to you!

FIONA. Christopher, have you taken leave of your senses?

DEWHIRST. *(laughs)* Oooh, get you!

CRADDOCK. There's fight in the old dog yet!

> **CRADDOCK** *exits.*

CHRIS. There sure is. I'm a middle-aged man. Avoiding you, Dewhirst? Give me one good reason why I'd want to do *that?*

> **DEWHIRST** *cracks him in the face.*

Oh. That's why.

FIONA. Yep. That's a pretty good reason.

> **DEWHIRST** *has seen the locket.*

DEWHIRST. What's this?

CHRIS. My – no, don't!

> *But* **DEWHIRST** *has pulled it from him and broken it already.*

DEWHIRST. Awww, is it broken? You going to have a tantrum, you little baby? Next time I see you: two Curly Wurlys. And a Texan. So long, puffter.

> *He exits.*

CHRIS. Oh shit. Oh no. Oh shit!

FIONA. *(looking at his nose)* That wasn't very clever, was it?

CHRIS. No… but then I aren't very clever… and if the locket's bust… I'm trapped! I want to go home! I've got a wife and kids!

FIONA. You're married?

CHRIS. Not for much longer if I can't get back. What if I'm stuck here forever… trapped in my thirteen-year-old self? Condemned to live my entire adolescence all over again?

FIONA. Calm down; let's look at this logically…

CHRIS. To regular detention and school gravy with skin on?

FIONA. Conan Doyle writes, 'When you eliminate the impossible, whatever remains, however improbable,

must be the truth.' So let's look at the facts, shall we?
The locket is the key…

CHRIS. To going round Clare Freeman's house when her
parents are away for the weekend, drinking cooking
sherry and…

FIONA. Christopher McCann, do you want me to help you
or not!?

CHRIS. Yes.

FIONA. Then focus – can we replace the locket?

CHRIS. No, the offer's all finished.

FIONA. And the only other locket is…?

CHRIS. Titch McCreavie's.

FIONA. Who's in Flumsworth?

CHRIS. Felsworth!

FIONA. Exactly. *(pause)* Well, that's where you've got to go
then.

CHRIS. Felsworth?

FIONA. And get Titch to give you his locket!

CHRIS. Me, go to Felsworth?

FIONA. Yes.

CHRIS. How?

FIONA. You got here. How did you do that?

CHRIS. I… I don't know, but – 1978 is real. Felsworth, it's
not exactly on the bus route, is it?

FIONA. Precisely my point. Felsworth isn't real, so try and
think surreally. Give me the comics, I'll read them
tonight… perhaps something will occur to me that
you've missed.

CHRIS. What shall I do?

FIONA. Well, try to connect with Titch, I suppose. Is
there anything you have besides the locket? A shirt, a
drawing, a… poster… er…

CHRIS *is completely still. Suddenly the life-size* **TITCH
MCCREAVIE** *poster pops into his head and he runs off
full tilt.*

Where are you going? I'll just see myself home, shall I?

But **CHRIS** *has gone.*

Madder than my uncle Clive.

Music. The stage is reconfigured.

Scene Ten

We are back in the bedroom. **GRANDAD** *is in the bed, snoring gently.* **CHRIS** *enters. The image of* **TITCH MCCREAVIE** *is on the wall.* **CHRIS** *stands before it. He puts one hand on the poster, clenches his eyes tight shut and concentrates. Nothing happens. He does so again. There is a rumble of thunder in the distance. He opens them sharply, looks up and around, tries it again, it comes in louder.*

CHRIS. *(whispers)* Titch! Titch where are you now…where are you when I need you…?

The thunder breaks and lightning cracks. **GRANDAD** *mutters in his sleep.*

GRANDAD. Mmmmn… bloody mice…

Lights up on another area of the stage, where **FIONA** *sits concentrating on the comic.* **CHRIS** *moves closer to the poster; speaks louder now.*

CHRIS. Come on… come on… something…

FIONA. *(a growing revelation)* The locket…

More thunder.

CHRIS. Anything!

FIONA. Christopher? Christopher!?

CHRIS. Titch! Please! Titch!

FIONA. Touch the locket…it has to be the key…

CHRIS *reaches out and touches the locket on the drawing on the wall. Lights through it, revealing* **TITCH MCCREAVIE**. *Music builds.*

TITCH. Christopher!

CHRIS. Holy shit!

> *Music louder and louder.* **FIONA** *looks around her. If we can source some kind of ground light – a birdie or a grill – to light up* **FIONA***'s face as she looks at the world of Felsworth, this would be the time.*

TITCH. Christopher…

FIONA. *(staring intently at the comic)* Oh my golly!

CHRIS. I hear you, Titch! I hear you!

> *Music and the storm form a real tumult.* **TITCH** *holds his hand out to* **CHRIS**.

FIONA. Is that…? No…!

> **CHRIS** *takes the leap and goes through the image on the wall. All is quiet.*

Wowzers!

Lights down.

Interval.

ACT TWO

Scene One

Lights up to discover **MR SELBY** *and* **TITCH** *onstage, frozen in a pose, as if part of a comic panel.* **MR SELBY** *is by the board outlining tactics,* **TITCH MCCREAVIE** *listening intently. The rest of the team is present via projection images. We hear a* **VOICE** – *it is a vocal representation of those words that used to appear in the top left hand corner of certain panels.*

VOICE. Matchday, at Felsworth Stadium. Manager Mr Selby is going through tactics…

SELBY. Today we play those fancy dan southern moneybags Southsea Hotspurs.

TITCH. Always a tough game. But don't you worry about a thing, Mr Selby! Promotion, this is our year!

SELBY. It's been my lifetime's ambition, Titch!

Freeze. Pose. Whenever the **VOICE** *is about to speak, there is a freeze.*

VOICE. But the wily fox of the dugout has another trick up his sleeve…

Movement.

SELBY. It's going to be an extra tough run in to the end of season. That's why I've made an important new signing!

TITCH. Terrific, boss! Just what we need. Who is he?

SELBY. He's a speedy inside forward. Just a kid, but with a nose for goal, an eye for a chance and an ear to the wind.

TITCH. Where's he from? Grimchester Albion?

SELBY. No.

TITCH. Blackton United?

> **SELBY** *shakes his head.*

Not Bruddersford blinkin' Rangers!

SELBY. No.

TITCH. You mean he's out of the orphanage same as where I was when you found me, boss?

SELBY. Not quite, but he's come from absolutely nowhere – I've signed him for a steal!

> *Enter* **CHRIS**, *in ill-fitting tight shorts. He gazes around at the dressing room.* **CHRIS** *is gobsmacked that he is actually here.*

SELBY. Welcome aboard, Chris McCann.

TITCH. Welcome to Felsworth, Chris!

CHRIS. Wow... *(grins at* **TITCH** *and* **SELBY***)* I used to imagine it...

SELBY. *(smiles)* Bless him, his feet haven't touched the ground since we signed him.

CHRIS. Now I'm actually *in* it... Felsworth!

SELBY. Every schoolboys dream, your chance to pull on the famous jersey! We had to rush the paperwork though to FA headquarters via our new state-of-the-art telex machine.

CHRIS. Wow! Telex machine, eh?! Hi tech!

> *Screen images spin their way into focus, of* **CHRIS** *– in comic panel image – signing for Felsworth, posing with a football etc.*

It's... It's... real... there's Howie Haddock! And... Lofty Towers, the lean and lanky centre half! And Taffy Evans, the erm... er... Welshman!

The other two have frozen. **CHRIS** *hasn't noticed.*

VOICE. Then...

> **CHRIS** *reacts to the* **VOICE**. *No one else does.* **TITCH** *is wearing his lucky locket.*

CHRIS. The locket.

TITCH. Ain't never played without it, have I?

CHRIS. No, but that's the real one! Titch, you're a lifesaver!

TITCH. What? That stuff at the bank? It was nothing. Happens all the time.

CHRIS. Course it does. Remember when those Kazamarian Separatists threatened to blow up Felsworth Nuclear Reactor?!

TITCH. Too flaming right I do!

CHRIS. Fortunately the Flame-haired Dynamo was right on hand to save the day!

> *All but* **CHRIS** *freeze again momentarily in comic frame pose.*

VOICE. Selby lays out his tactics...

> *And move.* **CHRIS** *looks around him again.*

SELBY. Okay, let's get down to business.

CHRIS. *(about the voice)* Who is that?

SELBY. We'll use the defensive, zonal, offside alternating sweeper, get-stuck-in-you-bunch-of-big-girls, flexible diamond formation...

CHRIS. Seriously; you didn't hear that?

SELBY. Three at the back, overlapping wingbacks, pushing up, in the hole, boot it miles upfield and all get after it, fluid pressing *European* gameplan. Got that, boys?

> *Freeze, all except* **CHRIS**.

VOICE. The players catch on fast...

> *Movement.*

CHRIS. There it is again!

SELBY. Any questions?

CHRIS. Yeah; who's th—

SELBY. Good.

TITCH. Genius, Mr Selby!

CHRIS. *(to himself)* One game can't hurt. Bugger it. *(to **SELBY**)* Okay, boss, I won't let you down!

SELBY. Good lad.

*All but **CHRIS** freeze.*

VOICE. Talk turns to the opponents…

*Movement. **CHRIS** has twigged.*

CHRIS. Oh! I've got it! It's the little bit of writing in the corner of each picture, isn't it?

***SELBY** and **TITCH** look at **CHRIS** with some concern, then press on.*

SELBY. Southsea Hotspur are no mugs boys.

CHRIS. *(pleased he's figured it out)* It's the little bit of writing.

SELBY. Even if they are owned by the filthy rich 53rd Earl of Southshire, who's also their star player!

CHRIS. *(grinning)* Come on!

TITCH. Why, he's so stinking rich he even mows his lawns with a Rolls Royce and waters 'em with flippin' champagne!

CHRIS. Love it!

*There's a freeze. **CHRIS** joins in.*

VOICE. At that moment…

*Enter **JACKIE**, wearing spectacles, an item of costume that markedly connects her with **FIONA**.*

CHRIS. *(commenting on the voice)* That's so cool!

TITCH. Babycakes!

JACKIE. Hello.

*The muted response throws **TITCH** a little, who was expecting her to throw her arms around him.*

TITCH. What's with the specs, cutey?

JACKIE. Oh, my eyes were getting a little strained.

TITCH. Oh no! Mr Selby, come quickly – Jackie's going blind!

JACKIE. Titch—

SELBY. That's terrible!

TITCH. Help me, Whiskers! Help me save the eyesight of my treacleface, who's got so much more to give! Only the Flame-haired Dynamo can save the day…

JACKIE. Titch, for heaven's sake be quiet!

This brings everything to a standstill.

Why is everything always about you?

TITCH. Because it just is, honey… I don't know why.

JACKIE. I've been thinking.

TITCH. *(pause, baffled)* Doing what, baby?

JACKIE. *(thinking)* Titch…about things in my life… I need to settle my mind.

She puts her hand to her temple, deep in thought.

TITCH. Your what, sweetcakes?

JACKIE. Could you please drop that patronising tone?

TITCH. Sure thing, honeyca–…sure thing! Thinking! Great! Is that why you're not at work today, at ultra modern, state-of-the-art skyscraper Felsworth Towers?

SELBY. In the heart of Felsworth's thriving technology quarter!

CHRIS. I believe it is, yes.

JACKIE. And why do you do that? Why do you insist on over-explaining everything? Have you any idea how *annoying* it is?

TITCH. Oh baby, come on, this is me, the Flame-haired Dynamo, I've never annoyed anyone in my whole life!

JACKIE. Oh, haven't you!?

SELBY. Jackie, sweetheart, it's team talk time. The Bert Selby tactical laboratory, the essential science of soccer made simple.

JACKIE. You're doing it again! You're always doing it! We need to talk, Titch.

TITCH. Sure, what about?

JACKIE. I need some time.

TITCH. How long? What to do? Hair? Nails? Shopping?

JACKIE. I've enrolled on a course at Felsworth Polytechnical Institute Of Education.

CHRIS. That's not in the comic.

TITCH. What is it?

JACKIE. It's the new building on the outskirts of Felsworth. I'm doing a course in Economics, Politics and Sociology.

CHRIS. *(slight panic starting to rise)* Neither's that.

SELBY. Boys! The team talk!

JACKIE. It's a place where women have a voice!

CHRIS. Or that.

SELBY. Now… their centre-half is a violent ex-convict…

JACKIE. And they have folk nights.

TITCH. They have what?!

JACKIE. Women singers, like Biffy Saint Jolie, Mary Ann Hipkins… and Katie Hedge.

CHRIS. Katie Hedge!?

JACKIE. They inspire me!

TITCH. *(gently)* Sweetheart… singing? Really? You sing like a broken exhaust pipe.

JACKIE. Stop putting me down! I won't have it! I want to test myself, find out about those Kazamarian Separatists at Felsworth nuclear reactor! Why they were prepared to risk their lives?! I want to do something important and change the world!!

TITCH. But why? When we can go shopping?

JACKIE. To hell with shopping. I'm interested in feminist theory.

TITCH. What's that?

SELBY. Femi Nisthery... ohoho, the Movaranian wing wizard of the 60s!

CHRIS. What? No, Mr Selby, I think you misheard...

SELBY. Why old Femi was a real *trickster* of the touchline!

JACKIE. *(at* **SELBY***)* What's he talking about!?

SELBY. With the feet of a dancing gazelle and the speed of a hungry cheetah!

JACKIE. Will someone shut him up before I hit him with the goalposts! I don't want to be just a footballer's bimbo girlfriend, or a secretary, I want to be my own boss, okay?!

TITCH. Jackie! Are you crazy? You don't want to be a top footballer's girl?

CHRIS. Whoa! Wait a minute! You want to—?

JACKIE. I'm sorry, Titch. It's not you...it's me.

TITCH. Babycakes! What are you talking about!?

JACKIE. No actually... it's not me... it *is* you.

CHRIS. Fiona...!

JACKIE. You say you're still Titch from the orphanage... and you ain't one of the nobs...but look at you...in your red sports car and ginger perm! Listen to the way you talk... I'm sorry, but you really are a nob!

Pause. No one knows what to say.

JACKIE. It's over between us.

TITCH. *(horrified)* Have you lost your mind!?

JACKIE. No, I've finally found it. The wedding's off.

She turns away from him, hand to face in strained expression. He is behind her in a framed image of deep shock.

CHRIS. Oh no. Oh Jesus.

TITCH. Jackie...?

JACKIE. I'm sorry, Titch.

She hands him the engagement ring and exits. **TITCH** *is dumbfounded, hands to his head, a framed image of deep angst! A pause.*

CHRIS. What was that? That doesn't happen!

VOICE. Titch is devastated…

CHRIS. *(to* **VOICE***)* No he isn't!

TITCH. Jackie!

CHRIS. Oh shit.

TITCH. Don't dump me! Please…!

CHRIS. Titch, don't worry; she loves you.

TITCH. *(crying)* Mr Selby… I can't… I can't….understand!

SELBY. What? The tactics? The offside rule? Spit it out!

CHRIS. Fiona! What have you done?

TITCH. *(between sobs)* She… called me… a nob!

SELBY. Crikey! Face it, son, she knows you best.

CHRIS. Fiona, I know you're out there!

VOICE. It's a real low point for the Flame-haired Wonder…

CHRIS. *(to* **VOICE***)* Shut up! You're not helping, you know! *(to* **MR SELBY***)* And you! Shouldn't you be inspiring the team like you normally do?

SELBY. Yes! Okay, er… Titch, I know your heart is breaking, and sometimes it seems like there's no going on.

TITCH. Yes, Mr Selby, that's it.

SELBY. Well stop it, there's a match on!

CHRIS. That's the best you've got? Are you kidding?

TITCH. *(through tears)* Boys, the match!

CHRIS. Oh. Okay.

TITCH. Let's get out there and get those two precious points!

CHRIS. Fiona… I'll deal with you later!

    CHRIS *and* **SELBY** *exit.*

VOICE. But…

    TITCH *sinks to his knees, and wails…*

TITCH. Jackie! Don't dump me!

A plaintive cry. The stage is reconfigured. Music.

Scene Two

The noise of the crowd comes in. **CHRIS** *lines up to play his first match for Felsworth Rovers. Via the combination of the panels and the live action onstage the game plays out. The live comic-style action is mirrored by the visual images of the comic frames. The speech bubbles tell us what's happening in the match.* **CHRIS** *and* **TITCH** *adopt comic-style poses as they speak.*

CHRIS. Come on, Titch, we need you mate!

SELBY. Titch! He's passed it to you!

TITCH. *(moping)* Huh? Blimey? Wot? Oh…

EARL. *(image/speech bubble)* I say, McCreavie seems distracted…

CHRIS. The Earl's robbed him!

EARL. Thanks awfully, old man!

CHRIS. Oh, no, no, no! This can't be happening!

The following are speech bubbles from the crowd

1. *Blimey. What's happened to McCreavie?*

2. *He's having a stinker alright.*

3. *Flame-haired Dynamo what's happened to you!?*

4. *Wet-haired Dishcloth more like!*

SELBY. Two-nil at half time…

TITCH. Normally Jackie would be up in the stand shouting 'Titch I love you!'

SELBY. Come on, boys, you can do it. Get back out there!

His Lordship shoots, scores, then very nonchalantly acknowledges the crowd with a series of very debonair waves.

CHRIS. Cripes, Titch! Tackle!

> *1.   The blinkin' Earl of Silver Stonkin Spoonshire's scored again!*

> *2.   He might be a toff, but he's a flippin good player too!*

> *3.   More than I can say about Titch Ma-flamin-creavie!*

> *Boos ring out around the stadium. The match finishes. They return to the changing room configuration.*

VOICE. The final score is four-nil to Southsea Hotspurs...

CHRIS. All right! Don't rub it in!

SELBY. *(to* **CHRIS***)* Decent debut, son, but Titch – what happened?

TITCH. Don't know, boss. I felt sure I was going to score two goals in injury time...

CHRIS. You were supposed to!

SELBY. At this rate we'll never get promoted. Not in my lifetime anyway. It's all slipping away, boys. Our dream. Please, Titch... we need you.

TITCH. I'm sorry, Mr Selby... everything in my life is upside down. Nothing makes sense any more. What do I do? Help me. Please!

SELBY. I... I don't know anything about things like that... I... know football and... football and... the war... sheepskin coats and wearing a trilby at the correct angle...and the Bert Selby Tactical Laboratory. And... football. Not—

CHRIS. Life?

SELBY. But I'll tell you this – if we don't win that last gasp, winner-take-all match against fierce rivals Bruddersford Rangers, we're going to be trapped in this division.

CHRIS. No! You go up! You do! It's a five-nil rout, and the Flame-haired Dynamo breaks Felsworth's all-time scoring record!

SELBY. That's the spirit, son, but... without Titch on his game, there's no chance. It's all over!

SELBY exits. **CHRIS** *and* **TITCH** *slump down on the benches.* **TITCH** *takes his locket off and looks at it.*

CHRIS. Titch... can, er... can I borrow that? Your locket?

TITCH. What?

CHRIS. It's a long story, but I need to go home. See my kids. And my wife, Debbie. We've had cross words recently, and I know I wind her up, but...you know, I can't help but wonder what she's doing? Who she's with? Probably wondering where I am... worried sick... I should think.

TITCH. That's what my Jackie was like. Worrying. Sighing. Looking up, like this:

He demonstrates.

What did I do wrong?

CHRIS. It's called life, Titch. Look, you've two choices – either you get behind her and go to some folk evenings, you know, beards, terrible teeth, all that...or you let her go!

TITCH. No!

CHRIS. Oh yes, 'cos sometimes that's what really loving somebody means... seeing that that they'll be better off without you... and sometimes – sometimes the hardest thing to do... is nothing...

TITCH. *(after a pause)* Well thanks for cheering me up. Yeah. What do you want my locket for?

CHRIS. I just need it to get home. It's hard to explain. Last time I saw her, she was going round to see that Simon. And I want to... I don't know, stop her, I suppose. How is anyone's guess, but—

TITCH. Borrow my locket?

CHRIS *nods.*

Of course you can't.

CHRIS. Oh mate, thanks, you won't regret it – I swear I'll take good—

Now he's finally registered the refusal.

Eh?

TITCH. No way. I've lost Jackie, not my locket too. I'm going.

CHRIS. Going where?

TITCH. None of your business! To get mind-bendingly, falling-off-the-stool drunk!

TITCH *exits.*

CHRIS. But...but... Titch! The Flame-haired Dynamo doesn't get drunk!

VOICE. The debutant was alone...

CHRIS. Yes, thanks.

VOICE. Don't shout at me, I'm just a narrative framework.

CHRIS. You're a bloody annoyance is what you are.

VOICE. You've changed your tune. You were calling me cool earlier.

CHRIS. That was before I got sick of you!

VOICE. *(mocks him)* Oooh get you!

CHRIS. Get lost!

CHRIS looks around, frustrated, then looks up and yells:

FIONA!?

Music. The stage is reconfigured.

Scene Three

Lights up across the stage on FIONA. She is in her bedroom, reading the comic. She jolts awake as if her reality/world has shifted. On the screen is a comic panel image of CHRIS, as FIONA sees him in the comic.

FIONA. Christopher!?

He looks up and around, trying to see her, but cannot.

CHRIS. Fiona!? Where are you?

FIONA. In my bedroom. I'm reading the comics you gave me. You're in them!

CHRIS. I know. Freaky.

FIONA. I take it all back! They're far more progressive than I thought they'd be.

CHRIS. Yeah; they are aren't they? All of a sudden! Couple of questions about that, actually.

FIONA. Fire away.

CHRIS. WHAT THE FUCK IS GOING ON?

FIONA. Sorry I couldn't read what you said then; there's a load of asterisks...

Christopher, are you swearing?

CHRIS. Of course I'm fff— *(calmer)* of course I'm blinkin' swearing! This is a mother-flippin' mess! I don't know what the flip's happened, but I swear to cripes you've got something to flippin' do with it!

FIONA. Me?

CHRIS. Okay, answer me this – how is it Jackie had your glasses on?

FIONA. Ask her, you're in Felsworth.

CHRIS. How is it there's a flippin' Polytechnic?

FIONA. Oh wasn't it always there?

CHRIS. No it flippin' wasn't!

FIONA. I'm not sure I care for your tone.

CHRIS. And I'm not sure I care for how the female characters are all suddenly self-aware! Or why Titch and flippin' Jackie aren't en-flippin'-gaged any more. It's an absolute Horlicks. The whole thing's gone to shoot.

FIONA. Guilty as charged! And a good thing too.

CHRIS. No it is not! You are messing with the... the... whole... equilibrium of *Felsworth*...

FIONA. You don't say.

CHRIS. The 1978 annual ends with Titch and Jackie getting married on the hallowed Felsworth turf! How the flip is that supposed to flippin' happen, if—

As **CHRIS** *continues to rant…*

FIONA. I've had enough of this.

CHRIS. – Jackie's dumped him and gone off to listen to Katie flippin' Hedge, the operatic queen of pop, and – eurgh!

*…***FIONA** *shuts the comic. Lights out on* **CHRIS***, who falls flat to the ground.*

(squashed voice) What have you done?

FIONA. Are you going to be nicer to me…?

CHRIS. Are you flippin' kidding? I don't have flippin' time for—

FIONA *slaps her hand down on the comic.*

Ow!

And again.

Ow!

And once more for luck.

Ow! Jeepers H Cripes! Pack that in!

Slowly **FIONA** *opens the comic. Lights up on* **CHRIS***, who stands. He's been battered.*

FIONA. Now are we going to behave…?

CHRIS *nods like a little boy.*

I'm starting to see why Debbie is so frustrated with you.

CHRIS. I never told you that.

FIONA. You didn't have to; I read it.

FIONA *flicks back a couple of pages in the comic. There on the screen is an image of Chris and Titch sat on the bench in the changing room, with a speech bubble* *coming out of Chris's mouth, which reads, 'My wife, Debbie – I know I wind her up.'*

FIONA. See? You can't say it's all down to me. Look at this—

*She turns another page and there's Chris with a think bubble above his head, reading, 'One game can't hurt! B****r it!'*

The second you made that choice you were altering their world too, so take some share of responsibility for once in your life.

CHRIS. Where have I heard that tone before?

FIONA. Besides which, I don't see what influence I'm having. I'm just out here, reading the comics, looking for clues, and – well… I've flicked forward a few issues, and… let's just say Felsworth is going through some changes…

CHRIS. Thanks to me… let's face it… I'm a flippin' hex!

FIONA. Au contraire Master McCann, I think it's all change for the positive.

CHRIS. Where's Titch now?

FIONA. Wait a minute… *(reads)* 'Turn to page 136 for the continuation of Titch McCreavie's desperate plight to save Felsworth's season'!

She flicks over a few pages. The action of turning pages tickles **CHRIS**, *and he laughs. Enter* **TITCH**, *drunk. There is a screen, projecting images, videos, dancing neon etc.*

Aha! Here it is…

FIONA *and* **VOICE** *together.*

FIONA/VOICE. Titch McCreavie drowns his sorrows deep in the dark heart of Felsworth's downtown sleazy disco bar quarter!

CHRIS. Where!?

FIONA. The legendary Felsworth Strip? I take it this is new?

CHRIS. Well I've never heard of it.

FIONA. This place finally gets interesting! There could be a punk band playing called Saskia and The Killer White Witches. It's what I'm going to call my band.

At once, in the distance, as if from a club over a PA we hear:

MC. *(off; distant)* Now, live on stage… Saskia and the Killer White Witches!

CHRIS. Can you stop doing that and just read it, please…?

FIONA. Okay… he's in Joey La Belle Belle's Disco Bar!

CHRIS. I'm not going anywhere called Joey La blinkin' Belle Belle's!

FIONA is getting into this. She jumps up as a disco beat comes in and lets rip.

FIONA. Ohh, Joey's a great character. He has a huge afro, and terrific flares! He says, 'Hi my disco peeps, I wanna see you get down! Bump those hips and lemme see that booty go boom baby…'

CHRIS. Yeah, alright, easy now, that's plenty thank you.

FIONA. Sorry Christopher. 'Now come on; get your skinny white bee-hind in there boy!'

CHRIS rolls his eyes and gets moving.

Scene Four

In comes a groovy disco beat, nasty neon lights flashing, images of dancing bodies on screen. Neon sign – Joey La Belle Belle's! CHRIS looks for TITCH. FIONA is in her bedroom reading the comics, helping him.

CHRIS. Where? Where?

FIONA. The VIP bar.

CHRIS wanders over. TITCH has a line of shot glasses in front of him.

CHRIS. Titch! Mate! There you are…

TITCH. *(wailing)* Oh Jackie!! What becomes of the broken-hearted, Christopher McCann?

CHRIS. What are you drinking?

TITCH. I don't know, but it comes in li-i-i-i-i-i-i-i-ittle glasses.

CHRIS *sniffs one.*

CHRIS. Tequila!

FIONA. *(sings)* Ba-dam-da-ba-da-bam-bam-baa…

CHRIS. Shut up, you!

The track 'Tequila' comes on.

Unbelievable.

FIONA. Sorry.

TITCH. Want one?

CHRIS. No, I'd rather a pint of real ale if there is one.

TITCH. Real ale? What's that?

CHRIS. The answer, no matter what the question. You don't know what real ale is?

TITCH. I didn't know what this was until this place turned up. Tequila!

CHRIS. What made you think of tequila?

FIONA. It's all my parents drink when they're depressed.

CHRIS. Tell 'em go easy, the 80s haven't even started yet. *Depressed*!?

TITCH *passes* CHRIS *a shot glass.*

TITCH. Welcome to the wrong side of the tracks.

VOICE. The pair drink long into the night…

CHRIS. Oh good. You're here as well, are you?

VOICE. Yes I am. Deal with it.

A central section in the bar now pivots, replacing a few shot glasses with many a ton of them. The music crossfades to 'Don't Give Up On Us Baby' – David Soul.

TITCH. *(wailing)* Ooohhhh Jackie!!! *(sings)* Don't give up on us baby, we've still got one more chance…. *(etc.)*

CHRIS. Oh pull yourself together! You're Titch, the Flame-haired Dynamo! Everybody loves you!

FIONA. What are you doing?

CHRIS. Trying flattery.

TITCH. *(wailing)* I don't want everybody, I just want Jackie…!

CHRIS. Forget Jackie! Aren't you the man who said that girlfriends come as standard with sports cars?

TITCH. Did I say that?

FIONA. Sure did, you berk.

CHRIS. *(to Fiona)* Ssshhhh!! *(to TITCH)* Come on Titch, you're the envy of Felsworth! And people like me, saddos who can't get a job – we look up to guys like you.

FIONA. What, self-obsessed, vain and utterly vacuous nincompoops par excellence?

CHRIS. *(to FIONA)* Button it. Please.

TITCH. You've got a job. You play for Felsworth Rovers!

CHRIS. No I don't… well, yeah I do, but… now I'm here it's… when I was thirteen the only thing I wanted was to be like you, and… then…

FIONA. … you turned into a middle-aged man with nasal hair?

CHRIS. Shut up! Just – I blame you for this! *(pause)* No I don't. I blame myself. And eBay.

TITCH. What the heck's eBay?

CHRIS. A good way to waste the day and spend a fortune you haven't got, on stuff you don't need, but hey, it's all progress! *(pause)* I bought a locket just like yours on it, but… it got broken.

TITCH. Like mine?

CHRIS. Yes. I'd had one before, but I threw it away when I was a kid, so…

TITCH. You are a kid.

CHRIS. I'm not.

FIONA. Debatable.

TITCH. Why did you throw it away?

CHRIS. I was angry. Someone lied to me. Someone I trusted. Turned out to be a... complete heel... and I never saw it coming.

TITCH. I never saw this coming. The betrayal...

CHRIS. The hurt...

TITCH. The feeling of emptiness...

FIONA. Is this what men are like?

CHRIS. *(to FIONA)* Shut up; we're bonding.

TITCH. The kind of pain that no sports cars, or playboy pad can heal...

CHRIS. You sound like Simon.

TITCH. You mean like from *Simon and Debbie?* I know.

A pause.

CHRIS. What?

FIONA. What?!

VOICE. Suddenly, on a huge screen at the back of the club...

The screen flickers. Suddenly it cuts to SIMON and DEBBIE at SIMON's house.

CHRIS *looks up at the screen.*

CHRIS/FIONA. *(together)* WHAT?

SIMON. I'm sorry Chris couldn't make it tonight...

DEBBIE. Are you...?

CHRIS. What the hell's this?

FIONA. It's not me.

TITCH. *Simon and Debbie?* It's this film, it's always on here, weird, futuristic, fantasy comic stuff; you know the type of thing.

CHRIS. What!? Debbie!

FIONA. Is that your wife?

SIMON. Truth is, since the divorce I've found it hard to really speak to anyone.

CHRIS. Shut up, then.

DEBBIE. No worse than being married, then.

SIMON. Apart from you.

CHRIS. What?

DEBBIE. What good would divorce do, I ask myself?

CHRIS. Divorce?

FIONA. Divorce?

DEBBIE. Couldn't be much more on my own that I am most of the time now.

SIMON. Chris is a great guy at heart.

DEBBIE. Chris is an overgrown schoolboy at heart. And not the fun kind.

TITCH. Chris! Hey, that's your name!

FIONA. Got it in one! The Flame-haired Genius!

CHRIS. Ssshhh; I'm trying to watch…

DEBBIE. He's just always somewhere else… spends his whole life running away. It's like he's still in his childhood… and do you know what's really annoying?

SIMON. That he prefers it there.

DEBBIE. Exactly! If he could muck about in bloody Felsworth with Titch McCreavie…

TITCH. And that's me! I'm famous!

FIONA. If his IQ was any lower you'd have to water him.

DEBBIE. And argue about storylines that appeared in Issue 242 in 1976…

SIMON. In microscopic detail?

DEBBIE. Yes!

SIMON. Right down to the slightest variation in the artwork, the colour and tonal texture?

DEBBIE. Yes! How come you know?

SIMON. It's men, Deb… Debbie… Deborah.

CHRIS. Oh, blinkin' is it? You smarmy clump!

SIMON. A lot of them, anyway...

DEBBIE. He wasn't always like this... that's the sad thing...

SIMON. I find it really hard...

CHRIS. What?

TITCH. Aye-aye; here we go...

SIMON. To look at you all day at work.

DEBBIE. He was funny, you know?

SIMON. Without wanting to come over...

TITCH. Here we go...

SIMON. And kiss you... just once...

FIONA. Oh dear.

CHRIS. What!?

DEBBIE. What did you say?

SIMON. What? That... I... ought to get another bottle of wine... I'm sorry, I shouldn't have said...

She leans over and snogs him.

FIONA. *(covering her eyes)* I can't look!

CHRIS. *(gutted)* Deb...?

DEBBIE. Yes, you should.

SIMON. I love you, Debbie. I have for a long time. You deserve better than him.

DEBBIE. Do I?

CHRIS. No you don't!

TITCH. Yes she does! That Chris sounds like a nerk.

SIMON. Come on. There's something I want to show you...

> **DEBBIE** *and* **SIMON** *leave.* **CHRIS** *is dumbfounded.*
> **TITCH** *is drunk and slurring. The film finishes with a*
> *'To Be Continued...' title card.*

CHRIS. Debbie! Debbie...

TITCH. What's wrong with you? It's only a film! More tequila, bartender!

FIONA. Christopher... I think I've figured out why you're here.

CHRIS. What?

TITCH. Fine…hic! I'll get it myself.

> **TITCH** *goes round the bar and gets a bottle.*

FIONA. I think you have to heed your own advice. You know, from earlier?

CHRIS. Why, so that I can face my own divorce? No way!

FIONA. Looks that way to me.

CHRIS. Not to me, alright!

> **TITCH** *is back with more tequilas.*

Titch, I need your locket now.

TITCH. Never… hic… ever. Hic. Comprende? My special lucky locket…is all I have left to get things back on track. Hic.

CHRIS. Maybe if you loosened a little less liquor? And stop saying *hic*! Nobody says *hic* when they get drunk!

TITCH. I do. Hic.

CHRIS. *(to* **FIONA***)* Fiona; can you just skip forward to where he gives me the locket?

TITCH. Who you talking to?

FIONA. I'll do my best…

> **FIONA** *starts looking through comics.*

CHRIS. I'm sorry… I hate to do this… I'm a peaceable feller most days but this is serious. Now give me that locket!

TITCH. Never!

> **CHRIS** *goes to take the locket from* **TITCH** *who resists. They end up in a fight. The screen images now project shots – which they mirror in heightened slo mo stage action of comic style fight – POW! THWACK! KERZONK!!*
>
> *Suddenly, in comes the flash of a camera, and onto the screens come the lurid newspaper headlines in the FELSWORTH INTERNATIONAL HERALD*

— TEQUILA TITCH! THE FLAME-HAIRED SAMBUCA IN SLEAZY DISCO BRAWL!

In the midst of all this, **FIONA** *has found something rather disturbing in a future issue.*

FIONA. What's this? Meanwhile, poor Mr Selby... Er ... Christopher? Hello...?

CHRIS. What? What? What?

FIONA. I think you better get to the hospital.

CHRIS. I'm not that badly hurt.

FIONA. It's not you... it's Mr. Selby...

CHRIS. Now what?

FIONA. Hold on – this may tickle a bit...

She flicks at the pages again. **TITCH** *exits, lights flash, the bar is struck, there's the sound of ambulances from the 1970s, and* **TITCH** *is back, wheeling* **MR SELBY** *in, wearing pyjamas and his hat.*

Scene Five

SELBY, TITCH and CHRIS in a pool of light. Venetian blind gobo. **FIONA** *still isolated in her spot.* **MR SELBY** *is looking at the newspaper on his lap, with the headline and image of* **TITCH** *and* **CHRIS** *fighting outside Joey La Belle Belle's Disco Bar.*

SELBY. I'm dying, boys.

TITCH. Mr Selby!

CHRIS. What the flip? This doesn't happen!

FIONA. It does now.

TITCH. What is it, boss?

SELBY. It's the old wounds from 1944.

The sound of artillery, shells landing, planes diving etc.

SELBY. Monte Cassino, 1944, fifty men storm a German machine post... only six survivors... I was lucky

I suppose... Why, the doc told me even then I'd not last another month.

TITCH. But boss, I thought he just said you'd never play football again?

SELBY. Titch, I'm no medical man, but I took that as an obvious side effect.

CHRIS. I don't believe I'm hearing this.

FIONA. I don't believe I'm reading it!

SELBY. I came through in the war... but not this time. I just want to live to see Felsworth Rovers promoted.

TITCH. Yes.

SELBY. Achieve our dream.

TITCH. Sir.

SELBY. Together.

TITCH. As one.

SELBY. No pressure.

TITCH. No no no.

SELBY. But it is my dying wish.

> **TITCH** *hugs him.* **MR SELBY** *has no idea what to do with this open affection.*

CHRIS. Mr Selby doesn't die! He's the manager for the entire series!

FIONA. That's true...only I can't find any Flame-haired Dynamo stories beyond this issue!

> *She holds up a comic.*

SELBY. I can feel it... it's all coming to an end.

CHRIS. What?

FIONA. The one after has a new story about a thawed-out caveman who goes on to be a champion boxer.

CHRIS. I can't believe it. What have I done? I've totally banjaxed everything in Felsworth! What can I do?

SELBY. We have one last match of the season to do it, boys...our arch enemies... Bruddersford Rangers, and it's a must-win for promotion!

FIONA. I guess you have to make a choice.

SELBY. Don't throw it all away, kid...life's too short. Think of all those kids at the orphanage, Titch...

TITCH. Yes, Mr Selby!

SELBY. Tell me you'll do it, boys! Go out and win it for the old man! If not. So be it, boys. I know you'll have tried.

TITCH. I'll try, Mr Selby... I want promotion...but what's the point of any of it...without Jackie?

CHRIS. *(nodding in agreement)* ...without Debbie? I understand, Titch, don't worry.

CHRIS *turns to see* TITCH *staring at him.*

CHRIS. What?

TITCH. You.

CHRIS. What about me?

TITCH. First... Jackie... now Mr Selby...?

CHRIS. Yeah... I... think I know why I came back to 1978 Titch...

TITCH. Ever since you got here, it's like some dark star has passed over me. All these years I've done nothing but score perfect goals, have perfect hair, eat delicious fondue and wear very small trunks at pool parties. Then you spring up out of nowhere, and bam!

CHRIS. Bam?

TITCH. Yes! Bam! Suddenly my life goes skiddly-wallop up in the air and I'm suddenly having all these...*feelings...*

CHRIS. I know... me too... that's good, right...?

TITCH. Is it?

TITCH *moves towards* CHRIS, *and not for a hug.*

SELBY. Boys... don't fight... please!

SELBY *starts to cough.*

CHRIS. Listen... I want to leave... just...

TITCH. Oh, you'll leave all right! You'll leave now!

FIONA. *(worried)* Christopher...?

SELBY. Lads...

More coughing.

FIONA. Christopher?

CHRIS. If I could just have—

TITCH. For the last time, you are not having it.

    TITCH *grasps the locket firmly in his hands. Thunder.*

    Go back where you came from. Beat it out of Felsworth!
You're not wanted here, okay!?

CHRIS. Titch; wait…

TITCH. Did you not hear me? Just… get… OUT!

SELBY. Titch…!

    *Coughing. Music. A reconfiguration featuring flashing
images, stuff we've already seen combined with other
cartoon icons. The wheelchair is removed, and* **SELBY***'s
hat –* **FIONA** *exits, as does* **TITCH***, and when the lights
settle* **CHRIS** *is onstage alone with* **GRANDAD***.*

Scene Six

    The **MCCANN** *living room in 1978.* **CHRIS** *is shocked to
find himself back there.*

CHRIS. Grandad! Jesus Christ!

GRANDAD. Was born this day.

CHRIS. What?

GRANDAD. Well, last night. Merry Christmas, Christopher…

CHRIS. Oh, yeah, merry Christmas, Grandad…

    He throws himself into his **GRANDAD***'s arms.*

GRANDAD. Steady on, kid. You'll have me over.

CHRIS. This is it then? The big one. They never told me.

GRANDAD. Join the club. Nobody tells me anything. Want
a Minto?

    He gets a paper bag out of his dressing gown pocket.

CHRIS. I never said goodbye to you…or understood what… was happening… to you.

GRANDAD. Well… if it's any consolation I don't understand it either, kid.

CHRIS. No. Guess not. But… Grandad…

GRANDAD. What, lad…?

> CHRIS *fixes him with a look.* GRANDAD *smiles slowly, a look of resigned acceptance.*

GRANDAD. Eh…come and open some presents.

> *Now the light spreads out to take in the whole house. The tree is lit, music plays, carols. Enter* JULIE, *who joins* GRANDAD. *They peer at* CHRIS, *expectantly. This is starting to get to* CHRIS.

JULIE. Merry Christmas.

CHRIS. Where's… where's dad…?

JULIE. Messing about with a retractable lamp in the kitchen. One of his mates got it him knock-off. I've always wanted one, so…

CHRIS. Oh yeah, if I pull it down in a couple of months don't go too mad, will you?

JULIE. You get weirder. *(shouting off)* Come on, bugger-lugs, we can't wait forever!

IAN. *(off)* Let him start; I'm nearly done! Open your presents, Christopher.

> CHRIS *looks at the presents and sees the one he wants. The flat, square-shaped one that is obviously the Venture Comic Annual. He picks the annual up, wrapped in Christmas paper, beams at it, savouring the magical moment of the paper coming off. Then he tears it off. It is a bright shiny bumper Venture Annual with a huge glossy picture of the Flame-haired Dynamo on the front. He beams at it, opens it slowly, takes in that glorious brand new book smell – holds it to his chest.* IAN *enters, watches him.*

IAN. Venture bumper Christmas Annual... with a huge extra special Christmas story of Titch McCreavie... the Flame-haired Dynamo and Felsworth's final push for promotion to the First Division.

JULIE. Have you read it?

IAN. I had a quick flick, yeah.

CHRIS. Magic. Pure... magic.

He flicks through it, and in comes the sound effects from the top of Act 1 as the different stories tumble out.

JULIE. Do you like it?

CHRIS. More than ever.

JULIE. What did you buy Fiona?

CHRIS. Oh... I offered to take her to see *Jaws 2*.

JULIE. Aww! You big softie, was she pleased?

CHRIS. Erm... I think she'll come round to it. Maybe I should have gone for a Woody Allen film now that I think.

IAN. Woody Allen? Left-wing nonsense. The Jewish Conspiracy, Christopher.

CHRIS. *(incredulous)* What!?

JULIE. Don't start today. *(to* **CHRIS***)* You like Fiona, don't you? I don't blame you, how sharp is she? God... makes me feel even dopier than I am.

CHRIS. You're no dope, Mum.

JULIE. I can't be right bright either, can I? Do you know what, I watch the Queen's speech every year...and five minutes after it finishes I can never remember a word she's said. Is it me who's thick or her that never says a bloody thing worth listening to!?

CHRIS. *(grins)* It's her.

IAN. Come on, then...

IAN puts his hand out, and **JULIE** *comes to him, and they dance to a Christmas waltz.*

There is an image of **IAN,** **JULIE** *and* **GRANDAD.** *This is the last time* **CHRIS** *ever saw them together. Enter* **FIONA,** *with a Christmas present. At first* **CHRIS** *doesn't see her.*

FIONA. Christopher.

CHRIS. Hi. Did you just…?

FIONA. Door was open. I've been worried about you. I came to see if you're okay?

They stand together and watch the scene.

CHRIS. Yeah. And no. Inside a week from now, one of 'em'll be dead… and the other might as well be…

FIONA. What?

CHRIS. Oh yeah.

FIONA. I had no idea.

CHRIS. Neither had I.

FIONA. That must…be…does it hurt?

CHRIS. Yeah. As much right now…as it ever did.

FIONA *takes his hand.*

Thank you. We go for a walk… you and I… this is… the day after tomorrow?

JULIE *notices* **GRANDAD** *looking a bit peaky. They stop dancing.*

JULIE. You all right, Dad?

CHRIS. And when we got back, they just said, "Christopher, your grandad's gone into hospital for a few days, love, he'll be looked after better there."

JULIE. Dad?

GRANDAD. I'm just a bit tired, stop mithering.

CHRIS. He didn't come out.

IAN. Come on, let's get you upstairs. Have a lie down, eh?

GRANDAD. Bugger off. I can do it myself.

CHRIS. I never said goodbye to him. Then, anyway.

GRANDAD *exits. He looks at* **IAN** *and* **JULIE.**

JULIE. Awww, hello, Fiona love. I didn't hear you come in. Merry Christmas.

FIONA. Merry Christmas, Mrs McCann.

JULIE. Look at you two! Where's that camera?

IAN. Bloody lovebirds, eh?

CHRIS. Yeah.

He wipes a tear away.

JULIE. Christopher, are you... alright?

CHRIS. Yeah... no...

IAN. You've changed.

JULIE. Have you been drinking Fiona's mum's homebrew?

CHRIS. *(laughs)* No...

IAN. Glad to hear it. You could strip wallpaper with that stuff. Just kidding, Fiona love.

JULIE. We should give Mrs Garbutt something for that.

IAN. What like? Penicillin? A police caution? Last rites?

JULIE *has gone for* IAN*'s jacket.*

CHRIS. Here it comes...

FIONA. Here what comes...?

JULIE. No, you know; a couple of quid, or...

She picks up his jacket. A book falls out, a bank book. She picks it up. She opens it, slowly looks from the book to him, and back again.

CHRIS. This.

JULIE. Ian...

IAN. Put it back.

JULIE. What...is this?

IAN. Just put it back. If you didn't look in people's pockets you wouldn't find things would you?

JULIE. You tell me what it is first?

CHRIS. Yeah, Dad, tell her.

JULIE. Christopher, go upstairs.

CHRIS. I think I'll stay this time.

JULIE. It's got your name on it...whose address is this?

CHRIS. Dad? Tell her.

IAN. Go upstairs! Put the book back.

JULIE. What have you been doing?!

IAN. Do as you're told just once for God's sake!

CHRIS. Or shall I tell her?

IAN. Christopher, go upstairs! Julie, give it all to me please!

JULIE. Not till you tell me what it is, and whose the address on the paying-in book and the cheque book is!?

CHRIS. Shall I tell her? About your other house...your other life...which is where you are at weekends and evenings all the time?

JULIE. Ian?! What's he talking about?

CHRIS. You know something, I went to look for you as soon as I could drive? Wanted to talk to you... to...see you one more time... and I did see you... in a semi-detached house on an estate in Gilberdyke.

IAN *looks gobsmacked, caught red-handed as it were.*

IAN. How could...

CHRIS. I looked through the front window and saw you sat there, fat, in a velour tracksuit and espadrilles, reclining on a bean bag watching *Live Aid* with a woman called Pat...and another kid... who wasn't me!? And you looked just as shifty and like you were lying to her...same as you always have us.

Silence.

JULIE. What?! Ian? Another... another kid?

IAN. Christopher, go upstairs and do as you're told!

CHRIS. No. See, I know now that you can't change the past. Okay? And you know what I've twigged? I wouldn't want to! Pissing off was the best thing you ever did. I believed every word you said as a kid, do you know that? Hook line and sinker, I bought the lot...we were gonna have a big car, house in Spain... like I ever cared about that.

IAN. Now you listen! I worked every day from leaving school, in an engineering works...everybody I knew went there... like lemmings. They might as well have put a chain on me! I hated every second of it, like a mouse in a giant mincing machine...everyday killed me a little bit more...it was all I was ever going to be... and they just shut the place down...so I got another job and that place shut down as well. I wanted to be the bloke in the suit, not the bloke in overalls...a somebody like my dad never was! I never knew it would be like this, ground into nothing... Do you understand me?

CHRIS. Yeah... partly I do. Partly. But I can't see the connection between that and having another woman. What? Just to make yourself feel better? Eh? Why? Don't wait a few days for my sake. Why hang about?

GRANDAD *enters.*

GRANDAD. What's all the bloody shouting about?

IAN *reaches for the bank book.*

IAN. Give it to me!

JULIE *holds it out of reach.*

JULIE. What about what I wanted, Ian? This is why you're out every night, this is why you're on *training* courses all weekend. You've lied to us all.

IAN. Not always. I'm sorry, Julie... I guess I felt I couldn't leave while your dad was poorly.

JULIE. Get out of this house...and never come back!

The Christmas carol is still playing. **CHRIS** *looks on as forlornly as he did that day in 1978.* **IAN** *heads for the exit. Finally he speaks.*

IAN. I'm sorry, kid. I never intended this, but life, work traps you, and all the things you set yourself up to be...out of reach... before you know it... your whole life's... like a big set of stories you've woven round yourself...you can't get free of...

CHRIS. All my life I thought I hated you... now I just feel sorry for you.

IAN. Goodbye, Christopher. I'm sorry.

Exit **IAN**. *Pause.*

GRANDAD. Another happy Christmas.

CHRIS. You all right, Mum?

JULIE. I will be. I... er... I'll just... er...

She's quite tearful.

GRANDAD. Don't cry about that gobshite.

JULIE. I'm not. Listen, I'll, er... I'll just get your grandad settled, and then... Have a bloody drink. Nice to see you, Fiona.

FIONA. You too, Mrs McCann.

JULIE *exits.*

GRANDAD. She'll be all right; I'll give her some of that homebrew. It's kill or cure, isn't it?

GRANDAD *exits.* **FIONA** *looks at* **CHRIS**.

FIONA. Wowzers.

CHRIS. Yeah. My own personal winter of discontent, this.

FIONA. All that stuff about the future, is that true?

CHRIS *nods.*

FIONA. Sorry about the locket.

CHRIS. Me too. But...

FIONA. What?

CHRIS. Well... maybe... maybe it's for the best, you know? Debbie deserves a better life than me, moaning and shutting off and living in an attic.

FIONA. You sure...?

CHRIS. No.

FIONA *hands him the present.*

FIONA. I forgot this. Merry Christmas.

He unwraps the present.

CHRIS. Oh. Surprise. *The Mayor Of Casterbridge...* by Thomas Hardy.

FIONA. It tells the tragic and cautionary tale of a foolish man who betrays the devotion of his wife and child and then bitterly regrets it as his life becomes a catalogue of catastrophe thereafter.

CHRIS. Yes. Thank you, I er... have got it now.

FIONA. I wondered if you'd like to still go to the pictures... with me?

CHRIS. What to see?

FIONA. *Jaws 2...* heck it's got a shark in it after all.

CHRIS. *(smiling)* It does indeed. Erm... wear some old trousers for that.

FIONA. Why?

CHRIS. A combination of hotdogs, Vimto, popcorn, a stressful Christmas and a rotten new year...

FIONA. Oh... I see.

Slowly they take one another in, top to bottom. Then she comes to him, and they are about to kiss. But he stops her mid-flow, puts his hands on her shoulders and holds her at bay.

CHRIS. Fiona... this absolutely never happened last time... when I dreamt of nothing else! And it really can't now. Believe me. But, thank you...then and now...even though you ran me ragged... you were the one ray of light.

FIONA. Do we stay friends? In...you know...?

CHRIS. I'll make sure of it.

FIONA exits as JULIE enters. They embrace. JULIE moves to where CHRIS is sat looking at his new annual.

CHRIS. I threw this away last time. This, and the locket; everything he ever got me. I walked out to the dustbin... and broke it in pieces.

JULIE. Just you me and now, sweetheart. We'll be fine.

CHRIS. You will be fine, Mum. You're strong... and still young... and prettier than I ever realised. You'll be fine. It's me that isn't.

JULIE. *(smiles)* Funny... so sweet... you talk like an old man sometimes. Come here.

CHRIS. Oh... one thing... I need to say this... If, say one night in the early 80s, I come down the stairs wearing eyeliner...

JULIE. Eyeliner?!

CHRIS. Hit me in the face and send me back up to take it off! Do not let me leave the house in it! Go for broke, you'll disown me, I am not your son, I might as well kill you now, really lay it on, I'm serious!

JULIE. What a Christmas.

CHRIS. I'll remember it, that's for sure. I love you, Mum... more than you know.

JULIE. Same. Oh same samey. Wrong in your head, bless you, but...

She exits. He is left alone. There is him and the Venture Annual. He gazes about, hint of the forlorn 13-year-old, lonely and bereft. He opens the comic for company. In comes the sound of the crowd...

CHRIS. Let's have a look, then. Contents – Jackson of the Jungle, blah-blah-blah, puzzle page – never bother with that – Sky Falconer and the Terror from the Transvaal – big Titch story throughout, Sergeant Craddock on the tank wheel again, poor sod...and...what the hell?

VOICE. Thank you, McCann – a Flame-haired Dynamo Mini Adventure...

CHRIS *flicks through the annual and finally, as at the start, in comes* TITCH MCCREAVIE.

TITCH. Cor blimey, Mr Selby's given us a stonking tough training session today! Only nine more miles to go! Still, we'll be fit as flamin' fiddles for the packed Christmas fixture programme!

JACKIE *enters.*

JACKIE. It's great that Mr Selby's let me train with you, Titch. Even though I've got a job as a relief worker for the Movaranian refugees.

TITCH. I just want you to be happy! And if that means being without me, well, so be it.

JACKIE. Oh Titch... I really respect you. Do one thing for me.

TITCH. What's that baby?

JACKIE. Never use the word babycakes ever again.

TITCH. Sure thing.

He takes the locket off.

JACKIE. What are you doing with that?

TITCH. Whiskers will always be with me, but this doesn't belong to me any more. It belongs to the man who helped me feel things... real things... big powerful... proper man things... he deserves it.

JACKIE. Who is he?

TITCH. He knows who he is...

JACKIE. But the match? Titch, you can't play without your locket. Bruddersford Rangers, the arch enemy! Last match of the season, a must-win for promotion! Two vital points!

TITCH. I'll play without it... I'll play with all my heart... that's my lucky locket now. In here! It beats for justice, and Felsworth Rovers. And all those poor little nippers down at the orphanage, and all the Movaranian children too. And Mr Selby. Don't worry, Mr Selby... I'm coming!

TITCH *finally turns to* CHRIS.

Thank you, Christopher McCann.

The sound of the crowd comes in. TITCH *holds the locket out,* CHRIS *takes it and puts it on. Thunder rumbles and lightning cracks...there is a sequence involving all actors and stage management except* DEBBIE *moving the set around* **CHRIS**, *even moving his chair back into place, until he is exactly where he was before the first shift. Lights.*

Scene Seven

CHRIS *is in the attic.*

DEBBIE. *(off)* Hello.

CHRIS. Debbie? Debbie!

The hatch is flung back and **DEBBIE** *enters. She and* **CHRIS** *look at one another a moment. As she speaks he goes to her and lifts her off her feet.*

DEBBIE. You've been up here…

CHRIS. Debbie! It's you! I'm… oh… Thank God!

DEBBIE. Have you been on the beer!?

He looks at her again, beaming.

CHRIS. No! Quite the opposite… oh, Debbie I'm…

DEBBIE. Are you alright?

CHRIS. Better than I've ever been! I'm bloody marvellous and so… so are you… well, that might be overstating it… about me, not you… I'm back! Praise be!

DEBBIE. Back from where? Have you been sat up here all night?

CHRIS. Erm… yeah… no… sort of… erm… ish… how was Simon?

DEBBIE. Don't start all this again.

CHRIS. No. Debbie, I've realized some things… this is hard, but… if I'm not the one to make you happy, then I want you to go and be happy.

DEBBIE. Happy? What's happy got to do with it?

CHRIS. Everything. I love you, more now than ever, but I blew it. Okay… here goes… I don't want you feeling stuck, trapped, caught in a thing, with me, that you're not happy in…that's not fair to you, to me, to the kids…

DEBBIE. What?

CHRIS. Yeah… it's not about me… it's about us… and what's right. I need to learn to do it.

DEBBIE. Okay… is this a version of… oh Debbie I love you, but it's not you it's me…

CHRIS. No I'm just… it is me… it's you as well… in a good way, I mean… we need to start again, Debbie… I need to start again… I've got something far more important and I know what it is…

DEBBIE. What is it?

CHRIS. You! Us. This. House, life, family.

She looks him up and down, smiles slowly.

DEBBIE. Chris, God knows you're stupid sometimes…

CHRIS. Yep.

DEBBIE. And you talk rubbish.

CHRIS. Spades of it.

DEBBIE. And a big kid and awkward…and some days I just want to hit you with a heavy object.

He glances about nervously, moves something that might qualify, like a cricket bat.

CHRIS. Right.

DEBBIE. But then there are other days, when I want to hug you so hard I'm scared you might break.

CHRIS. And today is…?

They hug.

DEBBIE. I loved you the day I met you; the day I married you… I love you now… you're in a rut; I'm going to stand by you. Okay?

CHRIS. Okay. So Simon's party…?

DEBBIE. He's a lovely guy, but I never realized there was so much about golf to bore someone with.

CHRIS. Did he… did he show you his ninety grand car?

DEBBIE. I don't care about stuff like that…

CHRIS. What do you care about?

DEBBIE. You… looking at me the way you used to… the way you're doing now.

CHRIS. Yeah; sorry about that; I think I'm getting a stye.

They smile at each other.

CHRIS. See all this stuff… Titch, Sergeant Craddock…

DEBBIE. Johnson of the Jungle…

CHRIS. Jackson!

DEBBIE. Him as well.

CHRIS. All going. eBay. First thing in the morning… it'll be gone in 24 hours and Christmas will be sorted.

DEBBIE. Christmas is tomorrow.

CHRIS. All right; well we'll have a stonkin' New Year instead. How about that?

DEBBIE. Have you got a temperature?

CHRIS. No, I've got a family…and I aren't letting it slip through my hands.

DEBBIE. Ha! Unbelievable! Wait till I tell Fiona.

CHRIS. *(confused)* Fiona?

DEBBIE. I Facebooked her earlier. She was saying you went really doolally one Christmas – wait till I tell her about this!

CHRIS. Fiona!?

DEBBIE. Your old school friend?

CHRIS. Where is she?

DEBBIE. Er… Paris?

CHRIS. Since when?

DEBBIE. You sure you've not been drinking? They've been there since Saskia was born…

CHRIS. Saskia?

DEBBIE. It's where she runs her design company.

CHRIS. Design company?

DEBBIE. You know all this! What's the matter with you? Oh, and she's found a publisher for her novel too. Looks like it's coming out next year. She's really chuffed.

CHRIS. Her novel!? Get in! Well done Fiona... I knew it, mind. Okay, eBay, here we go.

DEBBIE. Look, at least keep the annual and the locket... we'll manage.

CHRIS. No I'm gonna sell 'em both...that locket's worth a fortune. Titch McCreavie *himself* gave me that locket!

Pause.

DEBBIE. What?!

CHRIS. Joking. Obviously.

He hands her the annual, reluctantly. She watches him sceptically.

CHRIS. One thing... I have to know how it ends. *The Flame-haired Dynamo* story... just tell me how it ends.

DEBBIE. I thought you had this annual as a kid, knew it off by heart?

CHRIS. I did...but you hear stories different when you're a kid. I think it might have changed. Just...do they win?

DEBBIE. *(sighing)* What page?

CHRIS. 178. Right after the double page spread on the Harrier Jump Jet and before Craddock's Commandos... I think.

DEBBIE *looks.*

DEBBIE. Are you sitting comfortably? *(reading)* 'It's the final match of the football season, and Titch McCreavie is far from his usual self as Rovers are locked in a desperate last-ditch battle for promotion...'

CHRIS. I know all this. Just get to the match!

DEBBIE. All right, touchy. Er...

She turns a couple more pages. Unseen by DEBBIE, *enter* TITCH. *Followed by* SELBY *and* JACKIE. *The roar of the crowd comes in as they take up positions.* JACKIE *and* SELBY *on the touchline,* TITCH *on the pitch.* DEBBIE *and* CHRIS *are looking at the annual together.*

After a disastrous first half, Felsworth are two-nil behind.

CHRIS. No!

JACKIE. Ignore the two own-goals, Titch!

TITCH. I'll do my best.

SELBY. You'll need to do more than that, lad – today, you've got to outplay even your gramps! Argh!

> **SELBY** *winces in pain.*

JACKIE. Mr Selby – your medicine!

TITCH. Crikey!

CHRIS. I can't look. Do they make it? Does Selby live? Is Jackie now somehow in the medical profession?

DEBBIE. You tell me.

CHRIS. I can't! Turn the page! Turn the page!

> **DEBBIE** *turns the page. The whistle blows. The roar of the crowd.*

TITCH. Jackie? Book us a table at Luigi's Ristorante. Saving the day…

JACKIE. …always makes you hungry, oh Flame-haired Dynamo!

CHRIS. Brilliant!

JACKIE. Go, Titch, go!

TITCH. You just watch me!

DEBBIE. 'On the hour mark, Titch strikes! A bullet diving header…from a wicked whip of a cross…'

CHRIS. Supplied by Howie Haddock?

SELBY. Great ball, Howie lad.

TITCH. That's for you, Mr Selby!

SELBY. Get in, my son.

> *The following are speech bubbles, projected onto screens as in the opening scene.*

> 1   *McCreavie's back!*

> 2   *Go Flame-haired Dynamo!*

> 3   *We're still in this!*

DEBBIE. 'Five minutes to go, Titch picks the ball up in his own penalty area...'

JACKIE. He's past one man... past two...

SELBY. Past three more... he's nutmegged a dog on the pitch!

TITCH. Almost there...

JACKIE. Keep going, Titch!

1   *He's past the entire Bruddersford midfield!*

2   *Played a one-two off a steward!*

3   *It's like the ball's glued to his foot!*

CHRIS. Unbelievable!

DEBBIE. You're telling me.

TITCH. Almost there...

JACKIE. Why he's balancing the ball on his head—

SELBY. Both shoulders...

JACKIE. Hips, knees and bumps-a-daisies!

TITCH adopts a striking pose.

TITCH. Have that!

SELBY. It's in! You little beauty!

JACKIE. 2-2!

TITCH. That's for you, Jackie...

The sound of the crowd roar.

1   *One more goal and we're up!*

2   *Bruddersford are packing their defence!*

DEBBIE. And then, when all seemed lost... when nails were bitten to the quick and Mr Selby held his dying breath...

CHRIS. *(impressed with DEBBIE's reading)* That's the spirit!

JACKIE. Do something Titch! We're in the 14th minute of injury time!

TITCH. You mean... like this?

SELBY. An overhead bicycle kick!

JACKIE. With his weaker foot.

DEBBIE. From the halfway line.

CHRIS. Out on the touchline?

DEBBIE. Into the wind.

TITCH. Go on!

SELBY. It's flown off his boot... stopped in mid-air...

CHRIS. Yes? And...?

DEBBIE. ...hit the bar and went over.

> TITCH *head to hands; crowd huge groan.*

CHRIS. What?! You're kidding!

DEBBIE. *(grinning)* Course I am! It rocketed into the back of the net!

TITCH. Yeeeaaass!

JACKIE. Get in, my son!

SELBY. I love you, Titch McCreavie!

> *The final whistle blows.* JACKIE *and* SELBY *run to* TITCH. TITCH *looks up.*

TITCH. And that was for you, Christopher McCann.

DEBBIE. Wait a minute... he just said your name!

CHRIS. I told you... I didn't just read this stuff... I was in it!

> CHRIS *is standing looking at the three figures from his fantasy.* DEBBIE *shuts the annual. Their light fades, leaving them in the plain light of the set. They break from their freeze and turn to* CHRIS. DEBBIE *offers the book to* CHRIS.

DEBBIE. Want a last look?

CHRIS. No. Take it.

> *She kisses him. Music.* CHRIS *looks at the figures from his fantasy.*

So long, Titch. Mr Selby... and Jackie. I'll always think of you, but...time to let go.

> *They smile, and exit.*

Right, come on. Let's get cracking.

DEBBIE. Tonight?

CHRIS. No time like the present.

> **CHRIS** *smiles at* **DEBBIE**, *draws her to him. They embrace. Music swells. The image is replicated in a comic-style panel. And the words below are slowly, letter by letter drawn in...*

THE END